"Responsibility as destiny; we could hardly find a better motto for Václav Havel."
JAN VLADISLAV

Václav Havel: "arguably the greatest man—artist, anti-Communist dissident, philosopher-statesman—of the last half century"
NELSON W. ALDRICH JR.

Other Books by James W. Sire

CHRIS CHRISMAN GOES TO COLLEGE
DISCIPLESHIP OF THE MIND
HABITS OF THE MIND
HOW TO READ SLOWLY
JESUS THE REASON
SCRIPTURE TWISTING
THE UNIVERSE NEXT DOOR
WHY SHOULD ANYONE BELIEVE ANYTHING AT ALL?

Václav Havel

The Intellectual Conscience of International Politics

An
Introduction,
Appreciation
& Critique

James W. Sire

InterVarsity Press
Downers Grove, Illinois

InterVarsity Press
P.O. Box 1400, Downers Grove, IL 60515-1426
World Wide Web: www.ivpress.com
E-mail: mail@ivpress.com

InterVarsity Press® is the book-publishing division of InterVarsity Christian Fellowship/USA®, a
student movement active on campus at hundreds of universities, colleges and schools of nursing in
the United States of America, and a member movement of the International Fellowship of
Evangelical Students. For information about local and regional activities, write Public Relations
Dept., InterVarsity Christian Fellowship/USA, 6400 Schroeder Rd., P.O. Box 7895, Madison, WI
53707-7895.

ISBN 0-8308-2656-4

Printed in the United States of America ∞

Library of Congress Cataloging-in-Publication Data

Sire, James W.
    Václav Havel : the intellectual conscience of international politics: an introduction,
appreciation, and critique / James W. Sire.
        p. cm.
    Includes bibliographical references.
    ISBN 0-8308-2656-4 (paper : alk. paper)
        1. Havel, Václav—Philosophy. 2. Ontology. I. Title.
DB2241.H38 S57 2001
943'.704'3'092—dc2
                                                                            2001024415

20 19 18 17 16 15 14 13 12 11 10 9 8 7 6 5 4 3 2 1

17 16 15 14 13 12 11 10 09 08 07 06 05 04 03 02 01

To every politician—domestic or international—
whose passion is to live in the truth.

Contents

Abbreviations of Works Cited

Art	*The Art of the Impossible: Politics as Morality in Practice*
Disturbing	*Disturbing the Peace: A Conversation with Karel Hvízdala*
Garden	*The Garden Party*
Largo	*Largo Desolato*
Letters	*Letters to Olga: June 1979-September 1982*
Living	*Living in Truth*
Memorandum	*The Memorandum*
Open	*Open Letters: Selected Writings 1965-1990*
Redevelopment	*Redevelopment or Slum Clearance*
Selected	*Selected Plays 1963-1983*
Summer	*Summer Meditations*
Temptation	*Temptation*
Three	*Three Vaněk Plays*

Full publication data on these books can be found in the bibliography.

Preface

I have long been an admirer of Václav Havel. He came to light for me not as a dramatist or dissident or head of a foreign government, but as an intellectual, the author of an intriguing short quotation in a lecture I heard. *Who is this man?* I thought. Soon after, I was asked to give a lecture to students at James Madison College, at Michigan State University, on a topic that would relate to their main interest—public affairs. I had not yet settled on a topic for the lecture when, a few weeks later, I chanced on Havel's *Disturbing the Peace* in Colby's Bookstore in Berkeley. I bought it and read most of it on the plane back to my home in Chicago. I was hooked, first because I became fascinated with the man, and second because I now had my lecture topic for Madison College.

As I prepared my lecture, finding much in Havel's writing with which to agree and much to question, one of my colleagues suggested that I write him. *Ridiculous,* I thought. *Write the president of a country?* But eventually I came to think it a good idea. So off went a letter, the business end of which was to ask Havel if I could talk with him when I would be in Prague in a few weeks. Back came a response from Edá Kriseová—one of Havel's long-time friends, at that time one of the president's advisers and later his official biographer: "Mr. President is totally absorbed by state affairs of the country and has no time to devote to writing. We apologize . . . for not being able to take part in your project." I didn't think my request was that he take part in a project, but the answer was clear enough.

A few months later, *Crux,* a publication of Regent College in Vancouver, published my epistle as an open letter, which I sent once again to Havel, this time receiving no response.[1] Subsequently the letter was translated and published in Prague and, I understand, sent to him again. And again there was no response.[2] I went on to give my lecture at Madison College and not long after that also in Prague and elsewhere in Europe and the United States.

In the subsequent years I have paid attention to the news about Havel that has reached the United States, read his speeches that have been translated and often printed in the *New York Review of Books*, read his translated plays, and devoured each book by and about him that has emerged in English. Still, the closest that I have come to him physically was at the castle in Prague, where I had a friend take a snapshot of me outside his office door.

As I have worked on this book, the absurdity of my project has not been lost on me. Havel is his own best introduction. His own presentation of his ideas and of the details of his life is always more elegant—even in translation—than mine or that of others. So why introduce Havel and his work? First, to encourage whoever reads this book to read him! Second, to suggest where—given one's interests—one might begin. Third, to present the larger context into which his life and work fit. And finally, to identify, clarify and evaluate Havel's take on life, the key elements of his worldview. Havel the playwright-intellectual-dissident is now, of course, a practicing politician and has been for over ten years. Still, because a person's worldview is more foundational than either politics or drama, I have filtered my presentation of Havel's life, thought and political engagement through the grid of his role as an intellectual. My description of both his plays and his politics focuses primarily on his metaphysics, epistemology and ethics. I am especially interested in analyzing his concept of *Being*—what he often calls the "horizon of being"—and his most often repeated motifs, *responsibility* and *living in the truth*.

Despite the importance of these issues and the fascination Havel has provided for so many, there are at this time few substantial analyses of either his life or his work, at least in English. I have cited those that I have found most relevant. One book, the first and only independent biography of Havel to appear in English, needs special mention. John Keane's *Václav Havel: A Political Tragedy in Six Acts* is to be commended for providing substantial information about Havel's youth and his rise to political power that is otherwise unavailable in English. But Keane's book is flawed by inaccuracies, pretentious prose and, more importantly, a point of view biased against Havel. Keane sees Havel not as Havel views himself—a person thrust unintentionally into power—but as a deliberately manipulative politician. Keane also presents the life of the Czech dramatist-president in terms of the aesthetic form of *tragedy;* in the closing section of his book he even imagines a state funeral after Havel's death. Several reviews of Keane's book reinforce my own assessment and contain helpful biographical and interpretive information on Havel's life. I have listed these in the bibliography at the end of this volume.

Edá Kriseová, Havel's friend and presidential aide, wrote the first biography of him. For this she has received both commendation and criticism. The critics, she says, accuse her of writing "a pretty story, a fairy tale."[3] But she has borne that criticism as a badge of honor: "I am glad that I am guilty of writing fairy tales."[4] I would be less happy for this book to be considered a fairy tale. I offer it rather as an *introduction,* an *appreciation* and a *critique.*

This book is based almost solely on English translations of Havel's work. Fortunately, most of these works are well translated and are available in books and journals or on the web. Several readers with an intimate knowledge of the Czech language and Czech politics have read the manuscript and given me helpful advice. I would especially like to thank my Czech readers Mr. Michael Waloschek, Mr. Marek Mudrik, Mr. Pavel Raus and Mr. Karel Taschner; and my American readers Dr. Richard Pierard, Dr. Edward E. Ericson Jr., Dr. J. Budziszewski, Dr. Phillip Fisher and Mr. Fred Prudek.

If this volume sparks greater interest in the man and his ideas, if it leads its readers to heed Havel's call to responsibility, if it stimulates readers to respond positively to Havel's charge to "live in the truth," if it causes readers to reflect and assess the truth of their own worldview, most of my own goals for the book will have been realized.

Downers Grove, Illinois

1

The Unexpected Intellectual

Havel. A complicated man of mischievous irony and solid intellect, . . .
an idealist with strong spiritual inclinations, a playful thinker who speaks his native
language with precision and directness, who reasons with logic and nuance,
who laughs with gusto, who is enchanted with theatricality,
who knows intimately and understands his country's history and culture.

PHILIP ROTH, "A CONVERSATION IN PRAGUE"

VÁCLAV HAVEL IS ONE OF THE TWENTIETH CENTURY'S most amazing
people. In character, life and career he breaks all the molds we associate
with each of the six main categories into which he so obviously falls. He
is dramatist, humorist, intellectual, moralist, politician, statesman. We
may well ask, How can this be? Surely never before the combination of
these six—two perhaps, three maybe, four unlikely, but six?

The Unexpected Intellectual

In the United States Jefferson was intellectual, politician and statesman;
so was Benjamin Franklin. In Holland Abraham Kuyper was intellectual,
politician and statesman, as was Dag Hammarskjöld in Sweden. Intellectual and dramatist are blended in Bertolt Brecht, but while Brecht had
political and moral ideas, he was no politician. George Bernard Shaw in
England was a moralist, humorist, dramatist and intellectual, but not a
politician.

In whom are all of these qualities embodied? Stanislaw Baranczak
expresses amazement in his reflection on Havel as he became president

of the newly formed government of Czechoslovakia in late 1989. Let's say, Baranczak poses, that "destiny wanted the first president of post-Communist Czechoslovakia to be a writer, what kind of writer should that president be?" Would he not be "a genuinely good playwright with a genuinely strong set of moral convictions balanced by a genuine sense of pluralistic tolerance and a genuine sense of humor"? Indeed, says Baranczak, "In the middle of 1989, there happened to be one living and breathing candidate who matched this impossibly exacting description. His name was Václav Havel."[1]

Now add to these characteristics an attractive personality, a humility that is perhaps without parallel in politics, a keen insight into human nature and a desire to do good without claiming much for his own goodness. Václav Havel is indeed the unexpected intellectual who has become not only president of a country, but has striven to become the intellectual conscience of international politics as well.

There is an aura of euphoria in this brief description of Havel. Can anyone, especially anyone so engaged in public affairs, live up to such an assessment? Over Havel's first ten years as president his image has been tarnished by the many unrealized hopes of the Czech people, by some ineptness in his political maneuvering and by carping critics and politicians who are jealous of his position and power. As he moved into the last few years of his second and final term as president, he had, according to a *New York Times* journalist, come to be "regarded by many Czechs as something of a scold, or worse, a bit of a joke."[2] My assessment of Havel is that he falls between the two extremes of fairy-story hero and bumbling idealist. But that is to leap ahead of the argument. Before such a judgment can be justified, we need to consider some of the details of Havel's life and work.

The Intellectual Dramatist

I imagine that people looking back on their lives from the perspective of their sixties, which Havel now does, find much that seems both inevitable and unlikely. Surely no one would have predicted the details of Havel's life during his childhood and youth or even during his early career as a dramatist. But when in the fall of 1989 the king makers of Czech society

looked for a symbol of what they thought Czechoslovakia s
Havel was the obvious choice. For this dramatist, actor, writer-turned-
political-dissident had demonstrated the precise qualities that make for a
modest philosopher-king. How did he come by these qualities?

Václav Havel was born on October 5, 1936, to middle-class parents.
His father was a civil engineer. Havel himself might have turned out to be
a very rich man, had not Czech political reality intervened.[3] Denied
access to higher liberal arts education by the communist government
because of both his class and his "political profile," he found an outlet for
his intellectual curiosity in an association formed with other sixteen-year-
olds. The Thirty-Sixers, as they called themselves, met together to discuss
philosophy and literature. Havel even drafted a "short book on philosophy, which he called A First Look at the World,"[4] and he was privately
tutored in philosophy by J. L. Fischer.[5] Eventually he managed to be
apprenticed as a laboratory technician at Prague's Czech Technical High
School and passed the exams in 1955; he then took a further course in
economics and began to write and publish articles on literature and theater.

Failing acceptance as a film student at Prague's performing arts acad-
emy (AMU), Havel served in the military from 1957 to 1959 and fell into
the writing of a short play that was performed by his buddies and amused
his army cohorts. Again failing acceptance as a drama student at AMU, in
1961 he obtained work as a stage technician at Prague's ABC Theatre,
then later as a stagehand at the Theater on the Balustrade. He began to
write scripts and buried himself in the life of the theater. In 1964 he married Olga Šplíchalová, an usher at the Theater of the Balustrade. She
came from the working class.[6]

Havel's first serious play, The Garden Party, premiered at the Theater
on the Balustrade in December 1963. This absurdist drama is highly reminiscent of the plays of Eugène Ionesco and Samuel Beckett, as are several
of Havel's plays that followed (The Memorandum, 1965; The Increased
Difficulty of Concentration, 1968). The plays were well received in Prague
and were quickly translated and performed elsewhere in Europe and the
United States, winning for Havel a growing reputation as one of the best
rising dramatists. In May and June of 1968, Havel was feted in New

York on the occasion of the American premiere of *The Memorandum,* and he won the off-Broadway theater Obie award.

The Intellectual Dissident

It was not long before Havel's plays' implicit critique of Czech cultural reality under the communist regime became too trenchant, and the ubiquitous secret police increased their surveillance of him. In March 1969 Havel discovered a bugging device in his Prague apartment.

Over the next twenty years, Havel's life developed a pattern: he was watched, arrested, interrogated, detained, released, watched, rearrested, tried, incarcerated, released, watched, rearrested, tried again, reincarcerated and released.[7] When Havel was not in prison, he was not always able to work in the theater; in 1974 he spent nine months working in a provincial brewery. At other times during his periods out of prison, he wrote plays, some of which were performed in Prague, and some of which were performed only in Vienna and elsewhere outside Czechoslovakia. From 1977 to 1989 Havel spent five years in all detained or in prison. The charges, always dubious, sometimes completely fabricated, and never proven, focused on his dissident political stance. He was charged, for example, with "attempting to damage the interests of the republic" (1977), "obstructing an official in the exercise of his duty" (1978), "subversion of the republic," (1979) and "drafting a statement commemorating and denouncing the Soviet invasion of 1968" (1985).[8]

What did Havel do to merit these charges? He wrote and spoke against the Soviet occupation of Prague in August 1968; signed the "Ten Points" declaration "condemning the post-Dubček policy of 'normalization' [return to strict totalitarian control]" (1969); joined thirty-five Czech writers in presenting a petition asking for the release of all political prisoners (1972); wrote the major political tract "Letter to Gustav Husák," which circulated privately (1975); continued to write plays that were performed to critical acclaim outside Czechoslovakia but were barred from performance inside his country; helped found the Charter 77 movement (1977); joined eighteen others in founding the Committee for the Defense of the Unjustly Prosecuted (VONS) (1979); wrote the brilliant but politically incorrect essay "The Power of the Powerless," which circulated privately

(1978); and finally, from prison, wrote profound philosophically reflective letters to his wife, Olga, many of which circulated in private (June 1979 to September 1982).

Havel's final arrest took place at the end of January 1989, ten months before the Velvet Revolution, the bloodless fall of the totalitarian regime in Czechoslovakia. The police had found Havel in Wenceslas Square in Prague near a hastily erected memorial to Jan Palach, who twenty years before had set himself ablaze in protest against the Soviet invasion of Prague. Havel was not among those who had constructed the memorial. He was just standing by observing, amazed by the passion of those who were making their pilgrimage to the makeshift shrine. Havel was simply in the wrong place at the wrong time.

The Intellectual Politician

A few months after Havel's final arrest, the Berlin Wall came down, as did the barriers surrounding the entire Soviet Union. Czechoslovakian citizens were able again to have some control over their political destiny. On November 21, 1989, Václav Havel stood on a balcony overlooking Wenceslas Square and addressed hundreds of thousands of Czechs, calling them to fashion afresh a republic that would respect truth and exercise justice. Soon after that, he was elected by the Federal Assembly of Czechoslovakia as the first president of what came to be called the Czech and Slovak Federated Republics. He was elected to the same post a second time in July 1990. His role as a dramatist of the stage largely over, Havel turned his attention to the raw drama of politics, a setting in which he has not always performed successfully, as he has so often admitted.

Greatly lauded as he took office, Havel found himself facing difficulties whose solution lay beyond the control of his good will and good intentions. In his first months as president he collided with prime minister Václav Klaus, primarily over whether the Czechs and the Slovaks would continue to be united under a single political entity. Havel urged the formation of two republics in one federation; Klaus sided with Vladimir Mečiar in Slovakia and called for two separate republics. When Klaus and Mečiar won the day, Havel resigned his post as president in July 1992, choosing at first not to stand for the presidency of what he believed to be half a country. But he reconsidered and, despite the loss of some of his political support, he was elected in January 1993 to a five-year term as president of the Czech Republic.[9] Havel has been criticized for his failure to preserve the unity of Czechoslovakia and for the subsequent compromises that brought him back into the presidency.[10] In January 1998 the parliament reelected him by the narrowest of margins—one vote—and now he is serving his second and final five-year term as president of the Czech Republic.

Havel has also seen difficulties in his personal life. He is a chain smoker, and his health, a constant concern since the early eighties, has not been good. He has been in and out of the hospital with pneumonia (several times), chronic bronchitis, a ruptured colon, a hernia, a racing heartbeat and lung cancer. In December 1996 half of his right lung was removed. His wife Olga, long admired by the Czech populace for her support of social causes, died of cancer in January 1996. When he married actress Dagmar Veškrnova less than a year later, the people did not approve. Their displeasure has not been abated by her subsequent flamboyant behavior: she once whistled loudly in parliament "in a response to a speech by a right-wing politician who had sharply criticized Havel."[11] Quite unlike Olga's quiet sophistication, Dagmar's refusal to play the symbolic role of president's wife has not pleased the populace.

From Bourgeois Brat to International Hero

"That bourgeois brat!" an official of the communist Writer's Union said of Havel in 1967 as Havel once again "pestered the union officials" with a petition. Such was probably the opinion of many of the official's colleagues in the leadership of an organization that had been formed by the government to support writers who produced properly socialist literature. Combined in this phrase are references to Havel's "unfortunate" middle class heritage and to his penchant for discomfiting the comfortable. Middle class birth and tenacious independence of thought and action are sins in the tightly controlled world of a totalitarian state. They are also at least a small part of what makes Havel so extraordinary.[12]

Havel combines a warm, friendly public persona—characterized by a love for gossip, wine, women, rock music and cigarettes—with a highly sensitive moral conscience, a devotion to philosophic reflection that enjoys and needs solitude, and an appreciation for the ironies of public and private life.[13] This combination of qualities produces "what one of his acquaintances has described as the Havel Effect: from a distance he appears incredibly warm, intimate, and chummy; up close he's strangely opaque."[14]

> His political persona is uniquely effective. Havel is a sort of European Gandhi: shy and selfless, yet insuperably stubborn; seemingly egoless, yet devoid of moral doubt; cunning and even manipulative, but never toward his own personal ends; conscience-driven, but never condemnatory of those who aren't.[15]

Of all Havel's attributes, however, it is his courage that is most attractive. Whether as a minority protestor in the Writer's Union, a dissident with a powerful voice in the underground or a public proclaimer of sacrificial moral behavior, he has stood firm and often alone. He could easily have spent the creative years of his life as a writer in exile, as did his contemporary, novelist Milan Kundera. More than once he was given an opportunity to escape the tyranny of Czech communism, and his keepers would have been glad to let him go. But, with one significant exception that we will examine later, Havel has lived his philosophy. He has stood true to his deepest convictions. Even at the beginning of the new millennium as he is "imprisoned" by his position as president, he will not let go the responsibility he feels—not only toward his country or himself, but also toward "the order of Being" that encompasses us all.[16]

During these past thirty years Havel has been much more than an intellectual gadfly, a mere critic. He has been "living in the truth," putting his feet where his mind and conscience urge him to go. He is quite unlike Josef Gross, the hesitant, fearful, troubled intellectual he depicts in *The Memorandum.* Havel is strongly committed to human dignity, morally and politically, and he is intently engaged not only in theorizing about the human condition but also in aggressively living out the implications of his theorizing. His character commands attention to his philosophy. His imagination and his ability to embody his vision in dramas commands attention to his plays. We now turn first to his plays, then to the philosophy that underlies them and his entire life.

2

The Dramatist
as Intellectual

Were my plays regarded solely as a description of a particular social
or political system, I would feel that I had failed as an author; were,
on the other hand, they regarded simply as a portrayal of humankind
or of the world, I would feel that I had succeeded.

VÁCLAV HAVEL

Václav Havel is primarily an intellectual. As such he first wrote literary essays and plays, then political essays and finally intellectual speeches that have confirmed him as a voice of conscience in both domestic and international politics. He first attracted public attention as the writer and performer of his own plays in the mode of the theater of the absurd. These early plays were performed then banned in his own country while elsewhere in Europe and North America they were being performed and acclaimed. Havel then began to emerge as a public intellectual, a dissident whose ideas could not be tolerated in communist Czechoslovakia.

Havel insists that he never intended to become embroiled in politics, though his friends contest this. "I am not, I have never been, and I have no ambition to become a politician, a revolutionary or a professional dissident. I am a writer. I write what I want and not what others want me to write," he told Antoine Spire after his release from prison in 1983.[1] It is not hard to find many of Havel's other disclaimers of any interest in direct engagement in politics. If he has become a central figure in the political development of Czechoslovakia—which he has—this position, he insists, has been thrust upon him. His political life emerged, he believes, only because writers and musicians, especially of his generation, were banned. As he took up the cause of young musicians such as the Plastic People of the Universe, the result was inevitable: he became a persona non grata with the authorities and a major political voice. It was a voice limited to *samizdat* (underground) publication, yes, but Havel was a mouse whose roar was heard by cultured, politically astute citizens throughout Europe and beyond.

Whether or not Havel has been completely candid about his political aspirations, we will take him at his word for now and raise the subject again in chapter five. Here we will simply look at Havel as he claimed to see himself—as a playwright. When we examine his plays, it will become abundantly clear that Havel was intentionally a playwright of ideas; the very construction of his dramatic works reveals a profound understanding of human character and behavior, of social structure, and even of the presence (by its profound absence in the plays) of the transcendent. Implicit in all of the plays is a political subtext: the daily lived-in world of Czechoslovakia is absurd, not because reality is itself absurd, but because the current political system, attempting as it does to control the totality of human reality, is absurd. There is also a philosophic subtext: as human beings we are rooted in a quasi-divine Being to which we are responsible. But this is to leap ahead. First we need to examine the plays themselves. That is, we need to look at Havel the playwright.

Playwright is the proper word for Havel, better than *dramatist,* because it emphasizes the craft of his plays. All of his plays evidence an intense awareness of structure. Language, themes, ideas are introduced; stage actions are set in motion. Then these words, themes, ideas, actions are repeated, bent back on themselves and re-repeated. The enigma they often introduce has a half-dozen variations. To change the image, the changes are rung on a dozen bells. Clarity is confused. The straight is twisted. Then the confusion is clarified; and the twisted made straight but now at an angle.

"Beautifully constructed and brilliantly funny," wrote one reviewer. "Filled with 'sharply penetrating thought,' " wrote another.[2] Because we are focusing on Havel as an intellectual, we will pay more attention to the "sharply penetrating thought" than to either the "beautifully constructed" or the "brilliantly funny." It is that very context that makes the ideas sing and dance their way into the consciousness of the audience and onto the public stage of culture.

So how do these plays work to reveal and convey their philosophic and social reality? One fruitful way to answer that question is to notice that in each of his plays Havel creates what J. R. R. Tolkien called a secondary world, which exists over against the primary world of ordinary lived reality. The characters in his plays are not realistic imitations of real people. Rather they are secondary creations of Havel's imagination who live their lives in the world of the plays. They *are* what they show themselves to be by their lines, gestures and actions on stage.[3] Though Havel, as any dramatist must be, is intensely aware of the audience and yearns to engage them with the play, he never has the actors move among the audience; nor does he attempt to bring the audience onto the stage or into the action. Rather, the plays display the classical aesthetic distance of traditional dramaturgy.

One effect of this is to preclude any sense that the plays are didactic. Unlike the plays of George Bernard Shaw, Havel's plays have no introductions outlining and defending the ideas that will be presented in the play. Though several of the plays end in long speeches, these speeches are usually profoundly ironic; no actor ever delivers to the audience the moral of the story. No character is Havel. No speech sums up the meaning. Exiled Czech novelist Milan Kundera's description of his own work fits that of Havel as well: "I need to hear in the novel the voice that is thinking, but not the voice of the philosopher."[4] So even though Havel's plays are highly intellectual and deal with philosophic themes (ontology, epistemology, ethics, language), political themes (freedom of expression and action) and psychological themes (personal identity, fear and guilt), none of them can be reduced to one or more obvious messages. It is for that very reason that the plays are so powerful philosophically, politically and psychologically. Havel, the producer and the actors were jailed for them.[5]

Havel's plays present a secondary world that embodies ideas and actions that are like those of the primary world. They present characters who represent intellectual or moral views and who live and move in the world of the play, prospering and suffering because of the iron-clad laws of the secondary world. In all of Havel's plays that secondary world is a world that does not fit the measure of human nature.

The figures in the world of Havel's plays, on the other hand, do measure up to the status of being human. The plays get their intellectual and emotional power from the obvious disjunction: The characters are so human! The world they live in so absurd! Ah, yes, absurd—but very like Czech reality, indeed the social reality of any country behind the Iron Curtain. They are so like Czech reality that the plays were deemed too politically incorrect to be performed in their country of origin. But this secondary world is also enough like the world experienced by everyone everywhere that little stretch of the imagination is required of audiences that are not behind the Iron Curtain. Indeed, the plays have received accolades in Germany, Austria, Hungary, Canada and the United States. Havel gained his reputation first as a writer, then as a dissident because of what he wrote.

If Havel's plays are what upset the Czech political watchdogs and tweak the conscience of the rest of us, what sort of play does he write? Three sorts, says Phyllis Carey: "absurdist comedies," "morality plays" and "psychological-prison plays."[6] I suggest a parallel classification: plays focusing on ontological issues, ethical issues and psychological issues.[7]

Absurdist Comedies

The ontological "absurdist comedies" include *The Garden Party* (1963), *The Memorandum* (1965) and *The Increased Difficulty of Concentration* (1968), all performed in the small but important "off-Broadway" Theater on the Balustrade in Prague. The period represented by these plays ended abruptly on August 21, 1968, when Russian tanks entered Prague to stifle the new freedoms of discourse and association that had burst forth in the famous Prague Spring of that year. The first two of these plays are among the best known and admired of all Havel's dramatic works.

The Garden Party. The secondary world of *The Garden Party* is the working world of young Hugo Pludek. At home Hugo's parents try to prepare him for a successful entry into the world of work. Meanwhile Hugo plays a solo game of chess, taking each side in turn.

MRS PLUDEK:	Well, how goes it?
HUGO:	All right, Mum. (*Makes his move.*) Check! (*Changes sides.*)
PLUDEK:	How goes it?
HUGO:	Badly, Dad. Very badly, in fact! (*Makes his move and changes sides.*)
MRS PLUDEK:	How goes it?
HUGO:	Super, Mum! (*Makes his move.*) Checkmate!
PLUDEK:	You lost?
HUGO:	No, I won.
MRS PLUDEK:	You won?
HUGO:	No, I lost.
PLUDEK:	Come now. Did you win or lose?
HUGO:	Lost here—and won here.
MRS PLUDEK:	When you win here, you lose here?
HUGO:	And when I lose here, I win here.
PLUDEK:	You see, Berta? Instead of a total victory one time or a total defeat another, he prefers to win a little and lose a little each time.
MRS PLUDEK:	Such a player will always stay in the game. (*Selected,* p. 7)

It is precisely by playing both sides that Hugo learns to succeed and to remain "in the game." The problem is that when Pludek plays both sides he also ends up losing his distinct identity.

Such balanced, ping-pong dialogue is found in all of Havel's plays; here the closing of the dialogue is thematic:

MRS PLUDEK:	Life is actually a sort of a big chessboard. Does that mean anything to you?
HUGO:	It does, Mum! Without the warp you cannot bury the woof. (*Selected,* p. 10)[8]

Hugo's interpretation is cast in a twisted cliché, one of dozens in the dialogue. The ubiquitous clichés, in fact, have been called the chief character in the play. Hugo learns them first from his family, then from the working world that he quickly learns to command.[9]

Hugo's first job is with the Inauguration Service; his task is to inaugurate the liquidation of the Inauguration Service. Hugo sees this as a booby trap. How can the liquidation of the Inauguration Service be inaugurated by the Inauguration Service when it is itself being liquidated? Obviously, there will have to be training—both "inaugurational training of liquidation officers" and "liquidational training of inaugurators." Eventually "another training will have to be organized. Inaugurationally trained liquidation officers training liquidationally trained inaugurators, and liquidationally trained inaugurators training inaugurationally trained liquidation officers" (*Selected*, p. 35). Hugo and the Director of the Liquidation Service become enmeshed in an argument over the meaning of the words *but, fortunately* and *unfortunately* in a hilarious interchange. A lot of action takes place on stage with clothes being thrown into and out of a sack and a basket, and people crawling in and out of them. The scene ends as the Secretary *"steps into the basket as though it were a river. The lid slowly closes"* (p. 43).

As Marketa Goetz-Stankiewicz says, "At one moment words seem to provide the only logical element on stage, at the next moment they create complete confusion. The audience, unable to stop laughing, is taken through bounds and leaps of reasoning, across swamps of phraseology, as it watches sense turn into nonsense and nonsense into sense."[10]

The final scene takes place in the Pludek's apartment. Hugo, having totally taken on the identity of liquidation officer, has begun his work of liquidating the Liquidation Service. Now Hugo is looking for Hugo, not realizing that he himself is the Hugo he is looking for or that he has changed so much that he is no longer the person he was. The ensuing scene of nonsense badinage ends with Hugo's long monologue in answer to his father's question: "Listen, who are you, in fact?"(*Selected*, p. 49).

HUGO: Me! You mean who I am? Now look here, I don't like this one-sided way of putting questions, I really don't! You think one can ask in this simplified way? No matter how one answers this sort of question, one can never encompass the whole truth, but only one of its many limited parts. What a rich thing is man, how complicated, changeable, and multiform—there's no word, no sentence, no book, nothing that could describe and contain him in his whole extent. In man there's nothing permanent, eternal, absolute; man is a continuous change—a change with a

> proud ring to it, of course! Today the time of static and
> unchangeable categories is past, the time when A was
> only A, and B always only B is gone; today we all know
> very well that A may be often B as well as A; that B may
> just as well be A; that B may be B, but equally it may be A
> and C; just as C may be not only C, but also A, B, and D;
> and in certain circumstances even F may become Q, Y,
> and perhaps also H. (*Selected*, p. 50)[11]

Hugo babbles on and on about the flux of human reality: "I'm sure you
yourselves must feel that what you feel today you've not felt yesterday
and what you felt yesterday you don't feel today, but might perhaps again
feel tomorrow; while what you might feel the day after tomorrow you
may never have felt before" (*Selected*, p. 50).

Truth (epistemology) and being (ontology) themselves are slippery:

> Truth is just as complicated and multiform as everything else in the
> world—the magnet, the telephone, Impressionism, the magnet—and we
> all are a little bit what we were yesterday and a little bit what we are
> today; and also a little bit we're not these things. Anyway, we all are a lit-
> tle bit all the time and all the time we are not a little bit; some of us are
> more and some of us are more not; so that none of us entirely is and at the
> same time each one of us is not entirely; and the point is just when it is
> better to be more, and to not be less, and when—on the contrary—it is
> better less to be and more to not be; besides, he who is too much may
> soon not be at all, and he who—in a certain situation—is able to a certain
> extent to not be, may in another situation be all the better for that.
> (*Selected*, pp. 50-51)

Hamlet's famous question is posed again not in Shakespeare's noble
blank verse but in babbling incoherent prose:

> I don't know whether you want more to be or not to be, and when you want
> to be or not be; but I know I want to be all the time and that's why all the
> time I must a little bit not be. You see, man when he is from time to time a
> little bit not is not diminished thereby! And if at the moment I am—rela-
> tively speaking—rather not, I assure you that soon I might be much more
> than I've ever been—and then we can have another chat about all these
> things, but on an entirely different platform. Checkmate! (*Walks out.*)
> (*Selected*, p. 51)

Hugo has found a place in the absurd world of *The Garden Party,* but he has lost his unique identity. Hugo is now a mere bureaucrat in a world where the whole of lived reality has become "one huge office."[12] Says Goetz-Stankiewicz, "The circle is closed: man invents a system that in turn shapes him."[13]

Where, then do we stand as the audience in relation to the play? We grasp the nature of the secondary world; clearly it is secondary, created by the playwright. But we also see our own primary world mirrored in the play. Havel's Czech audiences "roll with laughter because they recognize how close scenes are to their daily existence."[14] But what about those of us who live in the free and rational world of democracy? Surely our world is not the world of Hugo Pludek. Or is it?

Long ago, on the basis of my own experience and observations, I formulated what I call Sire's Law of Ph.D. Temperament. Every person with a Ph.D. has this temperament in a measure greater than the population's average. The law reads: The holder of every earned Ph.D. has a very high tolerance for absurdity. Ask anyone with a doctoral degree, "Was there anything you specifically had to do to be granted your degree that had nothing whatsoever to do with your academic ability or personal qualification for the degree? How long did fulfilling this requirement take?" The answer is usually, "Oh, yes! Several things. It took months [sometimes years] just to meet these irrelevant requirements."

If absurd situations are frustratingly present in Western countries, they were rife in the countries of the Soviet bloc. Havel describes post-totalitarian society (Havel's term for the post-Stalin social system in Czechoslovakia) as a world "thoroughly permeated with hypocrisy and lies":

> The working class is enslaved in the name of the working class; the complete degradation of the individual is presented as his or her ultimate liberation; depriving people of information is called making it available; the use of power to manipulate is called the public control of power, and arbitrary abuse of power is called observing the legal code; the repression of culture is called its development; the expansion of imperial influence is presented as support for the oppressed; the lack of free expression becomes the highest form of freedom; farcical elections become the highest form of democ-

racy; banning independent thought becomes the most scientific of world views; military occupation becomes fraternal assistance. Because the regime is captive to its own lies, it must falsify everything. It falsifies the past. It falsifies the present, and it falsifies the future. It falsifies statistics. It pretends not to possess an omnipotent and unprincipled police apparatus. It pretends to respect human rights. It pretends to persecute no one. It pretends to fear nothing. It pretends to pretend nothing.

Individuals need not believe all these mystifications, but they must behave as though they did, or they must at least tolerate them in silence, or get along well with those who work with them. For this reason, however, they must *live within a lie*. They need not accept the lie. It is enough for them to have accepted their life with it and in it. For this very fact, individuals confirm the system, fulfil the system, make the system, *are* the system. (*Living*, pp. 44-45)

In a "post-totalitarian" society the impersonal system rules the personal world. In one Baltic country a computer expert from the West was assigned to study the possible use of computers in a major hospital. After he had completed his study, he presented his recommendations to the person in charge. His suggestions would have saved many hours of repetitious, boring work, many reams of paper and much money. "What do you think of this proposal?" he asked.

"It will never work," was the reply.

"Why?"

"Where would we put the stamp?"

When I first heard the story, I did not understand. Why would one need a postage stamp? No, I was told, not a postage stamp, a rubber stamp. Bureaucracy requires everything to be authenticated, sealed by the proper authority.

Bureaucracy, the red tape of the Red regime! In stores in communist Russia the customer stood in three lines—one to see the product, one to pay for the product, one to pick up the product. Polish exile Czeslaw Milosz likewise strikes out against its absurdity: "Bureaucracy is parasitic because its activities are unproductive; they do not shape matter directly. And bureaucrats have no more reason to glory in their financial security than the prostitutes or publicans of Israel under Roman rule."[15]

The secondary world of *The Garden Party,* exaggerated as it is, has its own logic, a logic not far from that of the primary world of all of us. Havel's Czech audiences saw the logic of their own world reflected in the absurdity on stage. And so did the authorities.

The Memorandum. The Memorandum has many of the same features as The Garden Party, including the Beckett and Ionesco-like absurdist form and the focus on the world of office work.

The secondary world of The Memorandum is set in three offices in one large organization. It opens with Josef Gross, the Director, reading an office memo he cannot understand because it is written in Ptydepe, a new language being adopted by the organization as an experiment in clarifying communication. In a hilarious sequence of events, Gross first loses his role as Director to Ballas, the Deputy Director, and then is further demoted to Staff Watcher, a job that requires him to work in a narrow hidden room with chinks in the walls that allow him to observe the work in five different offices. A more rapid sequence of events finds Gross back to the helm by the end of the play—nothing essential having changed either for the better or for the worse.

If cliché rules the world of The Garden Party, language itself controls the world of The Memorandum.[16] The Ptydepe language is a "scientific" invention designed to remove all ambiguity. Every possible thing, idea, emotion, expostulation has its own name, providing "greater precision than any current natural tongue" (Memorandum, p. 15). Lear, a teacher of Ptydepe, explains it:

> The significant aim of Ptydepe is to guarantee to every statement, by purposefully limiting all similarities between individual words, a degree of precision, reliability and lack of equivocation, quite unattainable in any natural language. . . . [A]ny Ptydepe word must differ by at least sixty per cent of its letters from any other Ptydepe word of the same length (and, incidentally, any part of such a word must differ in the same way from any Ptydepe word of this length, that is from any word shorter than is the one of which it is a part). Thus, for example, out of all the possible five-letter combinations of the 26 letters of our alphabet—and these are 11,881,376—only 432 combinations can be found which differ from each other by three letters, i.e., by sixty percent of the total. From these 432 combinations only 17 fulfill the other requirements as well and thus have become Ptydepe words. Hence it is clear that in Ptydepe there often occur words which are very long indeed. (Memorandum, pp. 16-17)

In fact, Lear says, the longest Ptydepe word is the word for a wombat; it has 319 letters (p. 17).

Gross spends most of the play looking for someone who will translate the memo for him. Finally he realizes that "any staff member who has recently received a memorandum in Ptydepe can only be granted a translation of a Ptydepe text after his memorandum has been translated. But what happens if the Ptydepe text which he wishes translated is precisely that memorandum? It can't be done, because it hasn't been translated officially. In other words, the only way to learn what is in one's memo, is to know it already" (*Memorandum*, p. 47). When Gross calls this situation a "vicious, vicious circle," he is threatened with dismissal from the organization. The fact is, however, that almost no one in the organization, including Ballas, who has overseen the introduction of Ptydepe, has been able to learn the language.

Eventually, Gross gets his memo translated. It dismisses the charges against him that had resulted in his removal from his post as Director, and it suggests that the Ptydepe program be "eliminated." By this time Gross just wants to be "a little boy again." He'd "do everything differently from the beginning" (*Memorandum*, pp. 69-70).

The play ends as Chorukor, a new language, is introduced. Chorukor operates on the opposite principle from that of Ptydepe. Here all the words are very similar to each other, and mistakes are not important. If one mistypes the name of the day on which a meeting is to be held, the meeting can always be held on the day typed. In his final speech Gross reflects on the epoch in which he lives:

GROSS: We're living in a strange, complex epoch. As Hamlet says, our "time is out of joint." Just think, we're reaching for the moon and yet it's increasingly hard for us to reach ourselves; we're able to split the atom, but unable to prevent the splitting of our personality; we build superb communications between the continents, and yet communication between Man and Man is increasingly difficult. . . . In other words, our life has lost a sort of higher axis, and we are irresistibly falling apart, more and more profoundly alienated from the world, from others, from ourselves. Like Sisyphus, we roll the boulder of our life up the hill of its illusory meaning, only for it to roll down again into the valley of its own absurdity. Never before has man lived projected so near to the very brink of the insoluble conflict between the subjective will of his moral self and the objective possibility of its ethical realization. Manipulated, automatized, made into a fetish, Man loses the experience of his own totality; horrified, he stares as a stranger at himself, unable to be what he is not nor to be what he is. (*Memorandum*, p. 86)

We might think that this is the voice of Havel himself. Indeed passages in his letters to Olga and in his speeches reflect the same point of view. But the speech does not function in the play in this way. Rather, these are the hopelessly self-justifying words of a man the essence of whose "self" lies exposed, an essence consisting of nothing admirable or even honest. Gross is living in a lie. His speech, while not so obviously cliché-ridden as those in *The Garden Party*, is just as trite, just as false. Why? Because, as Havel writes to Olga, "Truth lies not only in what is said, but also in who says it, and to whom, why, how and under what circumstances it is expressed" (*Letters*, p. 347).

It could be considered anachronistic to interpret *The Memorandum* in light of Havel's later reflections in prison. But such an interpretation, I think, would not be a distortion of Havel's conception in *The Memorandum;* nor would it be so in the case of *Temptation,* as we will see below. In fact, as M. C. Bradbrook wrote in 1984, "The author of *The Memorandum* is living out his play."[17]

In *The Memorandum* Gross is so caught in the web of potted language that truth cannot be uttered. No language—Ptydepe, Chorukor, Czech or English—can serve the truth under these circumstances. Those spoken to cannot hear the truth. Why? Because when people speak always to justify their own actions, rationalization has replaced reason. Moreover, the cliché is a sure substitute of illusion for reality.

No truth therefore is ever spoken in *The Memorandum*. The truth comes only as the audience realizes the disparity between what is said and what is shown, between the literal and the functional. Then they see the truth in spite of its absence. Or, better, in irony—the ontological vacuum of the play's secondary world—the truth is unveiled in the primary world of the audience's imagination. It is not the truth of a philosophic statement but of an aesthetic revelation of Being itself. Behind the facade of an absurd, confused, corrupt world, there lives, as Hopkins would say, "the dearest freshness deep down things."[18] Elsewhere Havel calls this substructure of human and natural reality by a variety of terms, including *absolute horizon* or *Being*, but in his plays no direct statement of the substructure's presence is ever made. Nonetheless, *The Garden Party* and *The Memorandum* are centrally ontological: the issue at the heart of both of them is neither what we know nor how we should live; rather, the issue is what reality is, what makes the universe tick. "What's It All About, Alfie?" could be their theme song.

Unlike Beckett, who never expects Godot to come, Havel, as we know from his *Letters to Olga,* has seen Being come. In his plays he projects bleak pictures of post-totalitarian society only to show the darkness that sets off the light. His comments on hope are relevant here, but we will postpone discussing them till later. A brief quotation will suffice: "People often ask me how my 'preposterous idealism' goes along with the fact that I write absurd plays. I reply that they are only two sides of the same coin. Without the constantly living and articulated experience of absurdity, there would be no reason to attempt to do something meaningful" (*Disturbing,* p. 114).[19]

In Havel's third and final absurd, ontological play the darkness continues.

The Increased Difficulty of Concentration. Initially *The Increased Difficulty of Concentration* is a difficult play to understand. It employs many of the elements of absurdist drama—sudden changes without transition, seemingly irrational behavior, consistency taken to the extreme of absurdity. The chief character, Huml, a social scientist, appears in sequential scenes dressed for the public or clad in a rumpled dressing gown. Three actions intertwine with no realistic relationship in time.

In the first action Huml dictates to his secretary a theoretical treatise on happiness. The text of his treatise is clotted, confused and pretentious. In the second action a team of researchers attempt to use Puzuk, a primitive computer that they treat like a human being, to gather evidence to help them achieve a "condensed model of human individuality" (*Selected*, p. 171). But Puzuk, like a human being, is temperamental: The room is either too hot or too cold.[20] When it seems to function properly and appears ready to ask questions, it asks for rest instead. When it finally does ask questions, they come too rapidly to be answered and are mostly nonsensical: "Which is your favorite tunnel? Are you fond of musical instruments? How many times a year do you air the square? Where did you bury the dog?" (p. 175).

The third action involves Huml's romantic attraction to every woman he sees. He has a mistress, Renata, to whom he vows love (promising he'll divorce his wife), but he also vows fidelity to his wife (promising he'll break off with Renata). Then while he is dictating to his secretary, Blanka, he makes a play for her.

There is always much erratic activity on the stage. People leave by one door and immediately appear at the opening of another. The characters move hectically back and forth across the stage. Doors open and characters repeat lines. Puzuk rattles off its questions and then in the uproar sets off its own siren. When Puzuk shuts down, the lights go out. Finally, in a long pretentious speech Huml articulates a philosophy of science that emphasizes the unpredictability and coincidental nature of human behavior and concludes by saying, "Hence, the fundamental key to man does not lie in his brain, but in his heart" (*Selected*, 180). Then, as if to bring back a sense of order in time, the play that began with Mrs. Huml announcing, "Breakfast!" ends with her announcing "Dinner!" (pp. 133 and 182).

The title summarizes the play; the audience recognizes in the confusion the increased difficulty not only of Huml's concentration but of theirs as well. *The Increased Difficulty of Concentration* played well off-Broadway in New York, and Havel won Obies for it and for *The Memorandum*.[21]

Havel's ontological focus is made explicit in his comment to his wife:

> All my plays . . . deal in one way or another with the theme of human identity and the state of crisis in which it finds itself. . . . The disintegration of human identity also means (psychologically) the disintegration of existential

continuity and therefore (philosophically) the disintegration of time (as an intensely experienced dimension of Being). I first tried to indicate this specifically in *The Increased Difficulty of Concentration* and it is presented consistently (nonthematically, or rather not as a "subject") in *The Mountain Hotel*, where various "poetic" tableaux of the crisis of identity (the interchangeability of characters, etc.) are linked—again "poetically"—to the disintegration not only of time, but of the whole space-time continuum. (*Letters*, p. 92)

And in another comment to Olga:

I think that the theme of human identity has always been intrinsically related to the phenomenon of theater. . . . Man in this context is not merely "what he is and, at the same time, what he knows he is," he is also a being that, aware of its own Being, represents or stands in for another being (or power) that knows of its own Being, thus acting as a medium for the manifestation of "Being in general" and retrospectively, therefore, for his own Being as well. (*Letters*, p. 290)

One can't get more thematically ontological than that. Unfortunately *The Mountain Hotel* (1976) has not, so far as I know, been translated. But all Havel's plays—even those forefronting the moral and the psychological—are nonetheless fundamentally ontological.

Morality Plays

We turn now to what Phyllis Carey calls the "morality plays"—*Audience* (1975), *The Unveiling* (1975) and *Protest* (1979), all one-act plays featuring Vaněk, a writer who is unable to support himself because the government places restrictions on what is suitable to publish. We will deal mainly with the first of these plays.

Audience. Havel tells us that he wrote *Audience* over a couple of days "to amuse friends," but it immediately took on a life of its own and was performed and appreciated by many others (*Disturbing*, p. 123).

The secondary world of *Audience* is a brewery. The play opens with the Brewmaster at his desk in his office, head in hands, snoring. Vaněk knocks and enters. He has been summoned by the Brewmaster, who, knowing Vaněk is a writer, tries to get him to supply information about himself, information the Brewmaster can pass on to the secret police to keep them off his back and to keep his job.

During the course of the play, the Brewmaster pours himself and
Vaněk many glasses of beer. When the Brewmaster goes out to relieve
himself—as he does often during the play—Vaněk pours the remainder of
his beer into the Brewmaster's glass. So Vaněk remains sober while the
Brewmaster gradually gets tipsy and finally falls dead asleep.

The Brewmaster does most of the talking, trying, not always cleverly,
to get Vaněk to "snitch" on himself. In the process, he tells Vaněk much
that Vaněk doesn't seem to know—or doesn't admit to knowing. In language filled with expletives, the Brewmaster even suggests that the
authorities are afraid of Vaněk: "You've got it made! You write your . . .
plays—you roll your barrels—and they can all go to hell for all you care?
What more do you want? The fact is, they're even afraid of you" (*Three*,
pp. 19-20).[22]

Vaněk wants to know what "they" want to know about him. But the
Brewmaster doesn't know the answer, and he thinks that Vaněk, who is
"what they call an intellectual" should surely know already (*Three*, p. 22).
The Brewmaster offers to take good care of Vaněk, to get him out of roll-
ing heavy barrels and into a cushy job; all Vaněk has to do is write
"somethin' down on paper for me once a week." He is under pressure to
get this or he will lose even this job; he's already lost a better position. But
Vaněk says, "I can't be snitching on myself . . . but it really is a matter of
principle, become a part of . . . part of a way of doing things I don't agree
with." (p. 23).

The Brewmaster says that Vaněk is being unkind to him, hurting him
by not cooperating. "You intellectuals. VIP's!" he blurts out. "You will
take a soft job but you won't put up with the frustrations I face. No way!
. . . Principles! Principles!" he thunders. "You fight for them because you
know how to sell them. I only get . . . busted for havin' principles!"
(*Three*, p. 24). The Brewmaster continues to rant, ending his speech by
saying, "What . . . do I ever get out of life? What's in it for me? What?" (p.
25).

At the end, the action briefly reverses. When Vaněk returns from
relieving himself, the Brewmaster is sleeping as he was in opening of the
play. The Brewmaster seems to have totally forgotten their conversation.
He wakes up and asks, "How's it going?" Vaněk replies with the words of

the Brewmaster from the beginning of the play, "Everything's all [fouled] up—" (*Three*, p. 26). Immediately the curtain falls.

Audience presents the powerless writer in a world controlled by a distant, incomprehensible force. The Brewmaster is no more in control than Vaněk is; he is caught in the web of the same system. In fact, Vaněk is more free because he is "living in the truth." The Brewmaster is quite willing to prevaricate to get a better job or to keep the one he has. Vaněk already has the most difficult job in the brewery. By living in the truth he stays in the worst job, but he keeps his dignity; if he snitched on himself, he would lose himself. So long as he maintains his integrity, he is not only living in the truth, but also demonstrating ironically the "power of the powerless."

But what are we to make of the end of the play? The roles of Vaněk and the Brewmaster reverse. It's Vaněk who complains and the Brewmaster who will listen. Has Vaněk capitulated? Will he ask the Brewmaster to accept his freely offered snitches on himself? Will he sell his soul?

Here is a simple illustration of Havel's use of irony and distance. Though Havel once worked in the worst part of a brewery, Vaněk is not Havel. The moral center of the story is not so much *in* Vaněk as it is above, below and behind him, that is, in Being itself—in the transcendent and absolute horizon that Havel says so much about in his letters to Olga. Havel respects the moral sense of the theater audience. Being will impinge on them; they will see what Havel wants them to see: that in the secondary world of the play neither character embodies the ethical good. Vaněk is far more attractive than the Brewmaster, but even though so far he is innocent, he is vulnerable to being seduced. Vaněk appears again as a character in Havel's *The Unveiling* and *Protest*. In fact, he becomes so attractive that other dramatists put him in their plays.[23]

The Unveiling. In *The Unveiling*, Vera and Michael have invited Vaněk to their newly decorated apartment to "unveil" to him the "things" they have finally been able to acquire as a successful bourgeois couple. The decorations are an expensive but grotesque collection of "sundry antiques and curious objects . . . an Art Nouveau marquee, a Chinese vase, a limestone Baroque angel, an inlaid chest, a folkloristic painting on a glass pane, a Russian icon, old handmortars and grinders" (*Three*, p.

31). They have also acquired a "wooden Gothic madonna" just because it fits a niche in the wall and, most importantly to them, an electric almond peeler. Vera says, "When you have what we call a place with character, your whole life suddenly—like it or not—acquires a certain face too—a sort of new dimension—a different rhythm, a different content, a different order" (p. 34).

What one sleeps on, what one cooks (it should be gourmet), where one travels to get the finest chocolates (it should be Switzerland), how one has sex (this they want to demonstrate to Vaněk): all these mold who one is. Possessions make the person. Vera and Michael tell Vaněk that the reason he is not writing is that he has given up the struggle. The "feeling of futility," he confesses to them, is due to his job in the brewery. Vaněk should stop working at the brewery and live like them—he should buy fine clothes for his wife, have her take cooking lessons, improve his sex life with her, travel with them to Switzerland.

Of course, the audience knows—and so should Vera and Michael—that if Vaněk began writing, he would have to adapt his writing to the wishes of the authorities. "Life is rough and the world is divided," Michael says, "and you are not going to change any of it" (*Three*, p. 46). Vaněk's struggle should not be with the system but with himself; he should change, and he could do so if he only followed their example. But Vaněk, always the taciturn listener, demurs. He becomes embarrassed by their vulgar behavior and tries to leave. Vera and Michael are offended by Vaněk's refusal to take their advice, and only after they beg and plead does he decide to stay. The play ends as the unveiling of their possessions proceeds.

The Unveiling is, of course, fraught with irony. Vera and Michael are right: possessions do make the person, but a person of no moral or intellectual depth. They mention, for example, that they would like Vaněk to meet their young son; they have decorated the apartment with the formation of his character in mind. But their son remains offstage. Things are more important than people.

Protest. In *Protest* Vaněk visits Staněk, who, like both Havel and Vaněk, is a writer. Unlike both Havel and Vaněk, however, he has written in a way so as not to be censored or imprisoned. Vaněk is trying to secure Staněk's signature on a petition to release a pop singer Javurek from an unjust imprisonment. Staněk commends Vaněk for his stance at first. He tells Vaněk that Javurek has gotten his daughter pregnant and that he would be pleased to see Javurek released. But when he finds that he is being asked to join Vaněk and his fellow dissidents, he begins to wheedle, inventing all kinds of reasons why he should not sign and trying to show that he is more noble than Vaněk.[24]

At the end of the play Staněk makes several long, convoluted speeches in which he rationalizes his decision. He suggests that Vaněk might have "talked more" than he should have when he was in prison, inferring that Vaněk made it more difficult for people like Staněk to live on the outside. Finally, the phone rings and Staněk learns that Javurek has been released. Staněk then gets the last word, and it is utterly ironic and disingenuous: "My dear fellow, you mustn't fret! There's always the risk that you can do more harm than good by your activities! Right? Heavens, if you should worry about this sort of thing, you'd never be able to do anything at all!" (Three, p. 75).

Vaněk the All But Silent seems at times like Švejk, the great locally acknowledged symbol of Czech national character created by Jaroslav Hašek in The Good Soldier Švejk. Švejk's is a "bumbling soldier and relativistic philosopher of compromise."[25] His picture hangs on the wall of the Brewmaster's office in Audience. Vaněk is not quite the holy fool that Prince Mishkin is in Dostoyevsky's The Idiot, nor is he a seemingly naive holy man like St. Francis. Rather, he is an original, a taciturn moral fool, human to the core.

Reflecting almost twenty years later on the three Vaněk plays, Havel writes:

Vaněk is really not so much a concrete person as something of a "dramatic principle": he does not usually do or say much, but his mere existence, his presence on stage, and his being what he is make his environment expose itself one way or another. He does not admonish anyone in particular; indeed, he demands hardly anything of anyone. And in spite of this, his environment perceives him as an invocation somehow to declare and justify itself. . . . The Vaněk plays, therefore, are essentially not plays about Vaněk, but plays about the world as it reveals itself when confronted with Vaněk. (Three, pp. viii-ix)

Even though the Vaněk dramas are profoundly ontologically grounded, Phyllis Carey is right to call them morality plays.

Psychological-Prison Plays

We turn now to the final category of plays, what Carey calls "psychological-prison plays." These include *Largo Desolato* (1984), *Temptation* (1986) and *Redevelopment or Slum Clearance* (1987).

Largo Desolato. In *Largo Desolato* Professor Leopold Nettles, a dissident intellectual, faces a moral and intellectual identity crisis. He has written a paragraph in his book *Ontology of the Human Self* that has offended the authorities. He is now being pressured to sign a paper saying he is not the Professor Leopold Nettles who wrote the book. If he will do that, the authorities will leave him alone. The pressure on the professor comes from all sides: from Bertram and two Sidneys (First Sidney and Second Sidney), who steal supplies for underground publication of his essays; from his mistress, Lucy, who says he has not been performing well sexually; from Marguerite, a new admirer who has fallen in love with him through his work; and from two secret policemen, First Chap and Second Chap.

Nettles realizes that if he signs this paper he will be declaring that "I am no longer me" (*Largo*, p. 29). Throughout the play, when he is alone on stage, he nervously watches the door of his living room, looks repeatedly out the peep hole, paces the floor, pops pills, exits to wash his face, returns, repeats these actions. Unable to come to grips with who he is, he delays signing the paper. Bolstered by Marguerite, who tells him that he has given her back the meaning of life, he decides categorically to refuse to sign the paper. "I'd rather die than give up my own humanity—it's all I've got," he declares (p. 55). But his moral fortitude comes too late. Nettles learns that his case has been "adjourned indefinitely" (p. 55). He then collapses and bangs his fists on the floor. He has been weighed and found wanting; he has lost his identity.

There is something of Havel's own experience in this play. Havel has said that after his release from a prison hospital, his time in a civilian hospital in Prague (in 1983) was a great joy to him. But after he was released from that hospital, he fell into deep "postprison despair": "At the same time, it is not an autobiographical play; it is not about me, or only about me as such. The play has ambitions to be a human parable, and in that sense it's about man in general. The extent to which the play was inspired by my own experiences is not important. The only important thing is whether it tells people something about their own human possibilities" (*Disturbing*, p. 65). Still, the play works out on stage a phase in Havel's own psychic life. He has objectified his inner struggle and, I would imagine, the struggles of many other dissident intellectuals. Moreover, in the psychological background of *Largo Desolato* is an earlier personal lapse that had already depressed Havel for years. In *Temptation* the issue surfaces again.

Temptation. *Temptation* is a retelling of the Faust legend. It is by far Havel's most complex play in form, structure, character and intellectual content. The summary here must therefore be more detailed.

The action focuses on Dr. Foustka, a research scientist, who is bargaining with Fistula (Mephistopheles of the legend) for insight into the world of the occult and reaps the consequences of this bargain. The Director of Foustka's institute is aware of Foustka's interest and warns him and his colleagues, in a speech riddled with clichés and pseudoscientific jargon, that some scientists are trying to conduct their work "in the spirit of an entire spectrum of mystical prejudices, superstitions, obscure doctrines, and practices disseminated by certain charlatans, psychopaths, and intelligent people" (*Temptation*, p. 13). So Foustka is well aware that if his research becomes known, it will get him in trouble.

Nonetheless, Foustka proceeds to put into practice what he has been reading about. As he draws a magic circle, Fistula, a smelly dwarflike man who claims to be a practitioner of the occult arts, offers himself as a subject for scientific study. Foustka agrees, telling Fistula that while he really has a scientific curiosity, he will pretend not to. When they shake hands, Foustka blurts out, "Man, your temperature must be fifty below zero," thus suggesting, in accord with Dante, Fistula's demonic nature (*Temptation*, p. 24).

Fistula offers to give Foustka help with his love life, in particular to give him access to the secretary, Marketa. Foustka is offended and says he needs no such help. At a party at the institute, Foustka talks to Marketa, explaining the anthropic principle and the case it makes for an intelligence in the universe. It works like a charm. Marketa is smitten with love.

In his mistress Vilma's apartment Foustka accuses Vilma of infidelity. She protests, asking him what he is afraid of. "My own self!" he replies. "Something's happening to me. I suddenly feel capable of doing all sorts of things that have always been alien to me. It's as if something dark inside of me were suddenly beginning to flow out of its hiding place and into the open" (*Temptation*, p. 43). As it turns out, Foustka is right about Vilma, and when her other lover appears at the door, Foustka brutally beats her.

At the institute the Director again says he knows that one of the scientists has been dabbling in the occult. Foustka admits that he is the one, but claims that he is doing so in order to scientifically investigate pseudo-science. His study "will be impartially and fully directed towards one goal alone: to discover truth" (*Temptation*, p. 54). The Director allows Foustka to proceed.

In Foustka's apartment Fistula claims credit for Marketa's attraction to Foustka, but only as a trigger: "If the devil exists, then above all he exists within our own selves! . . . I'm only a catalyst who helps his fellow creatures awaken or accelerate things that have long existed within themselves even without his help" (*Temptation*, p. 59). Foustka, says Fistula, was spouting cosmology only to manipulate Marketa's emotions. Foustka protests that he was saying only what he believes to be true. Fistula's response and the ensuing dialogue is central to one major theme of the play: "My dear Sir," Fistula says, "the truth isn't merely what we believe, after all, but also why and to whom and under what circumstances we say it!" (p. 60). This is almost a direct quotation from one of Havel's own letters to Olga. The notion played a role in the interpretation given to *The Memorandum* (see p. 32 above). Its role in this play is explicit. Foustka says Fistula is right; he has in fact lost his "moral vigilance" and given in to temptation, but doing so has "helped me discover a new inner light" (p. 61).

In a speech worth quoting at length, again Fistula turns the tables on Foustka:

I know that mechanism of thought rotation which you just demonstrated as well as I know these shoes of mine! We sorcerers call it the Smichovsky Compensation Syndrome. . . . When a novice first manages to break through the armor of his old defenses and opens himself up to the immense horizons of his hidden potential, after a little while something like a hangover sets in and he sinks into an almost masochistic state of self-accusation and self-punishment. Psychologically this emotional reaction is quite understandable: in an effort to mollify his betrayed scruples, almost as an afterthought, the novice mentally transforms the action through which he betrayed them into some sort of purifying lesson which he had to learn in order to become better. He makes of it, in short, a sort of small dance floor on which to perform ritual celebrations of his principles. It usually doesn't last long, and when he comes to his senses he recognizes what we, of course, knew from the start, but what we couldn't really explain to him; that is, the grotesque discrepancy between the dubious values in whose name he called down the most frightful punishment on himself, and the fundamental, existential significance of the experience that he is trying to atone for by means of this punishment. (*Temptation*, p. 62)

Fistula then sets Foustka against Vilma and refuses to give Foustka further advice on his now ruined love life.

At the institute Foustka learns that Marketa has tried to slit her wrists, and the Deputy reminds his colleagues that theirs is a pursuit of truth, echoing Fistula's comment on truth that I quoted above.

The truth must prevail, come what may. But for that very reason we must remind ourselves that looking for the truth means looking for the whole, unadulterated truth. That is to say that the truth isn't only something that can be demonstrated in one way or another, it is also the purpose for which the demonstrated thing is used or for which it may be misused, and who boasts about it and why, and in what context it finds itself. (*Temptation*, p. 66)

The Director again charges Foustka with "the study of what's known as occult literature" (*Temptation*, p. 69). Foustka admits to it, explaining that he did it to gather material for a brochure that would show the incoherence of mysticism itself.

Given that Foustka has actually practiced the occult arts, the Director points out a seeming contradiction:

It seems to me, Foustka, that it's high time to ask our pivotal question: how do you explain the fact that on the one hand you claim to have a scientific

viewpoint, and consequently must know that black magic is sheer charla-
tanism, while on the other hand you're trying to gain the trust of sorcerers
. . . [even making plans] to collaborate with him, and indeed to cover up for
him? (*Temptation,* p. 71)

Foustka makes a long, impassioned and reasoned defense, concluding
that his very commitment to science has obligated him to do so.

In his apartment Foustka accepts Fistula's proposal: He will offer Fistula a "cover" for his investigation of the institute while Fistula will be a
subject for his study. Foustka insists that he has not lost his "moral values"
(*Temptation,* p. 84) by doing this, but Fistula is again more perceptive:

> Don't you understand that if we're capable of playing around with the
> whole world, it is only and entirely because we depend on contacts that
> we're absolutely forbidden to play around with? To deceive a liar is fine, to
> deceive a truth teller is still allowable, but to deceive the very instrument
> that gives us the strength to deceive and that allows us in advance to
> deceive with impunity—that, you truly cannot expect to get away with!
> (*Temptation,* p. 86)

In the process of analyzing Foustka's ethical argument, Fistula becomes
something of an antitheologian, undermining the virtue of the Judeo-
Christian notion of forgiveness:

> That one (*points skyward*) overwhelms Man with a multitude of unkeepable
> commandments, and therefore there's nothing left for him but to forgive
> occasionally. The others, on the other hand, liberate Man from all those
> unkeepable commandments, and therefore, understandably, they are totally
> rid of the need, opportunity, and, finally, even the capacity to forgive. But
> even if that weren't so, they wouldn't be able to forgive the betrayal of the
> very agreement releasing all that boundless freedom. Why, such forgiveness
> would make their entire world collapse! But really, might not the obligation
> to be faithful to the authority which gives us that sort of freedom actually be
> the only guarantee of freedom from all obligation? Do you see what I mean?
> (*The Temptation,* p. 86)

Fistula is saying, in essence, that what Foustka has tried to do is self-refut-
ing. While claiming to search for truth, Foustka is rejecting the search for
truth by rejecting the foundation on which such a search could be con-
ducted.

Again Foustka tries to justify his deceptive actions: "The only reason that I was able to make the promise was because I was determined right from the start not only *not* to keep it, but at the same time to cleverly use the position it gained for me—naturally in close consultation with you—for our purposes and to our advantage" (*Temptation,* p. 87). But Fistula has understood! Foustka indicates in this speech (note the "I" that becomes "our") that he has come over to the side of the demonic, or at least is feigning to have done so.

Fistula says he made the charge he did in order to give Foustka a chance to renege on his commitment to the occult. But Foustka did not do that. Fistula says it's lucky that he is not really the devil, for the devil would not have allowed Foustka to seem to betray him as Fistula has allowed Foustka to do. But this is, of course, the big lie. Actually Fistula—and the audience too by now—know that Foustka has just made an irretrievable commitment to irrationality and evil. Fistula shakes hands with Foustka and exclaims, as Foustka did earlier, "Man, you must be a hundred below zero!" (*Temptation,* p. 88). The deal is consummated: Foustka has become Fistula.

At the institute's mock witches' sabbath Foustka wears the traditional stage costume for Faust, and everything comes unraveled for him. Marketa, who is dressed like Ophelia, sings Ophelia's death song and ignores Foustka. The Director tells Foustka that Fistula (who "never lies") has been an agent working for the institute and that he has known from the first about Foustka's attempt to deceive the institute. Foustka recognizes his moral collapse; he is a beaten man. The witches' sabbath goes into high gear, Foustka's cloak catches on fire, and the fire and smoke clear the theater.

Temptation is such a complex play that I will not attempt here to reflect on every theme that cries out to be noticed. We will leave until other chapters a discussion of personal identity, the implicit concept of transcendent Being, and the nature of the universe. Now, however, we will look more deeply at the interrelated themes of truth, guilt and fear.

I agree with Phyllis Carey's designation of *Temptation* as a psychological-prison play. For years Havel has been dealing with what he considers to be a personal lapse; he has been trying to make his peace with a mistake that he fears has marred his character.

At the center of Havel's system of values is the concept of "living in the truth." Havel stressed this notion in "The Power of the Powerless," one of his two most important essays distributed underground among dissidents. Living in the truth involves four main subconcepts: (1) that truth is ontological (there is a truth to live in), (2) that this "truth" is epistemological (a statement of the way things are), (3) that this truth is ethical (it is the way things should be) and (4) that this truth requires a lifelong and total commitment without prevarication or withdrawal. Czeslaw Milosz's description of "trying to live well" can be taken as a gloss on Havel's living in the truth: "It means not sinning in thought against the structure of the universe, which is meaningful. One sins by falling into hallucinations, by absolutizing impermanent values, by despising our mind, which leads toward a mathematical ordering of cause and effect."[26]

If one lives in the truth, one lives in light of what one believes is true whether it is believed by others or not, whether it is convenient to do so or not. Indeed, the consequences of living in the truth while also living in a post-totalitarian society may not be pleasant. In "The Power of the Powerless," his most profound social critique, Havel imagines what might happen to the greengrocer who one day ceases to post in his shop the required political slogan: "He will be relieved of his post as manager of the shop and transferred to the warehouse. His pay will be reduced. His hopes for a holiday in Bulgaria will evaporate. His children's access to higher education will be threatened. His superiors will harass him and his fellow workers will wonder about him" (Living, p. 55).

Living in the truth, however, involves more than merely refusing to post a political slogan one does not believe. And it is also different from merely stating propositions that one holds to be literally true. The context has a great deal to do with whether what one does or says is living in the truth or living in a lie. This is what Havel discovered during his first time in prison in the spring of 1978. He submitted a request for release, cleverly—he thought—framing his petition so that he would obtain the release without violating his commitment to the truth. But the authorities used the petition to undermine his credibility with other dissidents. Havel writes about this in a letter to Olga: "I came out of prison discredited, to confront a world that seemed to me one enormous, supremely justified rebuke. No one knew what I went through in that darkest period of my life: . . . there were weeks, months, years, in fact of silent desperation, self-castigation, shame, inner humiliation, reproach and uncomprehending questioning" (*Letters*, p. 348).

Havel was so profoundly grieved over this that after his release he courted arrest so he could redeem his lapse of wisdom as well as demonstrate to his dissident colleagues that he had not given up his fight for human rights. He continues: "I felt best of all, relatively speaking, in prison: when I was locked up a second time I caught my breath a little, and the third time—until today—I have finally managed, or so I hope, to overcome it" (*Letters*, p. 348).

From this experience Havel claims to have learned two things, one about truth and one about failure. About truth: "Truth lies not only in what is said, but also in who says it, and to whom, why, how and under what circumstances it is expressed" (*Letters*, p. 347). And about failure:

> I've only now begun fully to realize that the experience wasn't just—from my point of view, at least—an incomprehensible lapse that caused me a lot of pointless suffering; it had a deeply positive and purgative significance, for which I ought to thank my fate instead of cursing it. It thrust me into a drastic but, for that very reason, crucial confrontation with myself; it shook, as it were, my entire "I," "shook out of it" a deeper insight into itself, a more serious acceptance and understanding of my situation, of my thrownnesses and my horizons, and led me ultimately, to a new and more coherent consideration of the problem of human responsibility. (*Letters*, p. 349)[27]

These comments in "The Power of the Powerless" and in Havel's letters to Olga find their ironic parallel in *Temptation*. Havel himself admits that "the truth is not simply what you think it is; it is also the circumstances in which it is said, and to whom, and how it is said. . . . [This] is one of the themes of *Temptation*" (*Disturbing*, p. 67). What he does not say but is easy to see is that his second lesson—about failure—is also a theme of *Temptation*.

When Foustka admits that he has lost his "moral vigilance" and given in to temptation, he claims to have learned an important lesson. "Your dark designs have helped me discover a new inner light," Foustka tells Fistula (*Temptation*, p. 61). The failure was fortunate. But Fistula is quick to make a rejoinder—one we do not find in *Letters to Olga*. He calls Foustka's revelation "the Smichovsky Compensation Syndrome." That is, Foustka is a psychological textbook case. He has simply performed a typical act of self-justification; he has "mentally transformed" his betrayal into a "purifying lesson," which he is deluded into thinking has helped him "become better" (pp. 61-62). This won't last long, Fistula says. Maybe for both Foustka and Havel, Fistula is right.

I think that what drew Havel to the Faust theme was his own prison experience of writing a document that while "sort of true" could be easily manipulated into something "entirely false." He had been used by the system. *Temptation* helped him work through the implications of what he had done. The irony is that Havel's own understanding of his loss of integrity is labeled by Fistula as the Smichovsky Compensation Syndrome: self-justification. Perhaps in *Temptation* Havel reopened the wound in his psyche in order to cleanse it and to bring healing. It's not clear to me that the play actually accomplishes this. It's as if living in the truth requires Havel to live in the truth of his guilt without being able to live in the truth of forgiveness. Perhaps that's because in Havel's overall grasp of reality, there can be no forgiveness. Perhaps Being is unable to forgive. We will discuss this topic later when we examine Havel's worldview more fully.

Redevelopment or Slum Clearance. Another of Havel's complex plays with several well-developed characters who represent or take moral or cultural positions is *Redevelopment or Slum Clearance*. The issue in question is the transformation of a medieval town overlooked by a castle. Its population is two thousand "souls, as they used to call them" (*Redevelopment*, p. 51). All of the action is set in the main room of the castle.

Albert, an young architect, is a romantic idealist who perceives his own conscience as the "voice of a Supreme Being." He is dead set against the redevelopment project (*Redevelopment*, p. 20). Ulch, another architect, is a social engineer and a true believer in the project. Mrs. Macourkova, a third architect, just echoes the views she thinks most safe at the time. Bergman, the director, is depressed about his life and follows the letter of the law on his job even though he would like not to. The Special Secretary to whom Bergman answers is a complete functionary who follows the redevelopment plan with rigor.

In addition, there are Renata, a young and pretty secretary, and Luisa, a matronly architect who has not lost her sexual vigor. They combine with various of the men to add a romantic or at least sexual dimension to the drama. Plekhanov, another architect, is the moral center of the play. He is aware of the misery in both the village below and the castle of architects above, and he wants to preserve the past while opening the way to the future. Throughout the drama he plays a violin, reminding the characters—and the audience—of the beauty of the past. In the end, however, he is the one who can no longer cope with the insanity of the redevelopment plan. Unexpectedly, he imitates the action of an earlier noble resident of the castle, committing suicide by jumping out of the tower.

One of the major themes of the play is the relationship between architecture and society. Bergman ends the play with a final word on that theme:

> Let us vow never again to connive in the "redevelopment" of the souls of ourselves or others. Our mission is not to dance to the frivolous beat of an incompetent conductor, but to hold fast to the truth we have found, and dedicate ourselves to the work we have begun. Only thus shall we be true to the moral legacy of this terrible and unexpected death. Only thus can we respond with dignity to the warning voice which calls even now from the depths of the castle moat. (*Redevelopment,* p. 64).

But this speech is as cliché-ridden and inane as all the others, for life among the architects and villagers will not change. Plekhanov's "voice from the depths of the castle moat" has now replaced Albert's "voice of the Supreme Being." Indeed, if there is a more reliable statement about this theme, it is Plekhanov's comment on the human condition: "True, [with our redevelopment plans] we'll spread misery among the people down there, but then indirectly they're responsible for spreading misery up here; architecture is well called the mirror of society. In other words we're applying the well-known Law of Universal Misery Exchange" (p. 52).

The play ends with Luisa grabbing the model of the castle, which has sat on the table since the beginning of the play, and thrusting it down on Bergman's head.

Redevelopment or Slum Clearance interweaves several of Havel's by now familiar themes: personal identity, human ineptness, transcendent Being, language, bureaucracy, power and truth. Here he also focuses on technology (as he did in *The Increased Difficulty of Concentration*) and on social engineering itself.

Every one of Havel's plays is an intellectual drama. Ideas play in, out and around the characters, their actions and dialogue, the stage setting, and the occasional music. Despite the shift in focus from ontological to moral to psychological, each play advances in complexity the elucidation of Havel's basically unchanged philosophy of life, his enduring world-view. If we look for radical shifts in fundamental perspective over Havel's twenty-odd years of play writing, we will not find them. "Steady as she goes" seems to have been the ruling word at the helm of Havel's intellec-tual ship. This becomes even more clear when we look at the contents of the ship, as we will do in the next chapter.

3

The Intellect
of the Intellectual

Consciousness precedes Being, and not the other way around,
as Marxists claim. For this reason, the salvation of this human world
lies nowhere else than in the human heart, in the human power to reflect,
in human modesty, and in human responsibility.

VÁCLAV HAVEL, ADDRESS TO THE UNITED STATES
CONGRESS, 1990

IMAGINE THAT YOU ARE PERCHED ON TOP of a railway signal pole over-looking a vast set of railway tracks. On your right and left and ahead of you are the tracks that come from the railway station behind you. As you look down the tracks, you see them stretch toward the horizon. Though some seem to link with others and some to disappear completely, they remain individual as they extend away from the station and away from you, finally meeting only at the horizon. The field of tracks is so wide that the sun makes some tracks glow more than others. But one thing is certain, every track is leading in the same direction; not one branches off to the left or right; the destination of all of them is identical.

This is a picture of the works of Václav Havel in relation to the world-view that they all embody. There is, it seems to me, little deviation in the direction of Havel's work from his early plays to his latest political speeches.[1] Some of the works are more significant than others, some are more complex, some are reflective, some hortatory, some written in the clotted prose of a prisoner who needs to sneak philosophy out of his cell in the guise of personal letters, and some written in the witty badinage of absurdist drama, but all lead to *living in truth* in *a final reality* that holds all of us *responsible* for our thoughts and actions.[2]

In this chapter I examine Václav Havel's worldview, or what we might call the intellect of the intellectual. A *worldview* is a person's fundamental understanding of the way things are in the world, a set of presuppositions, or assumptions, that the person holds about the basic makeup of the world. The presuppositions may be true, partially true or entirely false, and they may be held consciously or subconsciously, consistently or inconsistently.[3]

Essentially, a worldview answers seven questions: (1) What is fundamental reality? (2) What is the nature of the external world? (3) What is a human being? (4) What happens to a person at death? (5) How can anyone know anything at all? (6) How can a person distinguish between right and wrong? (7) What, if anything, is the meaning of humankind's sojourn on earth? In this chapter we will examine Havel's worldview, and in the next, his political philosophy. Both will be assessed in the chapter after that.

In making this examination we are taking a risk—the risk of violating Havel's own disclaimer: "I have never created, or accepted, any comprehensive 'worldview,' let alone any complete, unified, integrated and self-contained philosophical system or beliefs which, with no further adjustments, I could then identify with and which would provide answers to all my questions" (*Letters*, p. 190).[4] But for our purposes a worldview need not be "comprehensive," or "complete, unified, integrated and self-contained," or set in concrete, never to be modified. In fact, a worldview need not even be consciously held. Each of us has a worldview, whether we know it or not. That is, each of us acts from a perspective that reflects a commitment to a "way the world is." It is the constant backdrop to the decisions we make every day. Moreover, Havel is quite conscious about his answers to each of the seven worldview questions posed above. We do not have to guess at what he thinks, though we will certainly see that he is less than confident that he has reached closure on the answers. Even his claim that he has no "self-contained system" is challenged by what he writes in the Letters 129 to 144 (*Letters*, pp. 319-75), where he does present, in complex philosophical language, a somewhat formal exposition of his worldview.

Being: The Absolute Horizon

The first and most important element in any person's worldview is the answer that is given, implicitly or explicitly, to this question: What is fundamental reality? That is, what is so basic, so foundational, that nothing more basic exists? Carl Sagan, for example, opens his television series *Cosmos* with this bold statement: "The cosmos is all that is or ever was or ever will be."[5] For Sagan the really real is the space-time continuum, the subtle and complex combination of matter and energy. This is a view, by the way, that Havel understands and soundly rejects.

Early in his intellectual development Havel seems to have grasped a notion of fundamental reality that, while it becomes richer, does not vary much from the first hints of its appearance. Its features combine aspects of Christian theism and Heideggerian metaphysics. Havel's most common term for this fundamental reality is *Being*. Like the word *God* in Christian theology, the word *Being* is strewn helter-skelter throughout Havel's prose works. When the concept is not mentioned in these texts, it is always in the background, giving depth to all of Havel's life and works.

What Havel means by Being is easily misunderstood. The concept, which acts in Havel's worldview like the concept of God in Christian theology, is not a very exciting term for anyone's god. In his presentation of his worldview in his final prison letters, Havel begins not by explaining Being but by explaining how the human self begins to recognize Being (without necessarily understanding it) and begins to come to terms with it. This is the phenomenological approach. In phenomenology one begins not by answering the first worldview question, about fundamental reality, but by analyzing one's conscious perceptions. These mental acts become the given data of one's philosophy; from them the nature of external reality emerges. Although this procedure can lead to skepticism, for Havel it does not. Rather his phenomenological analysis ends in a strong affirmation of Being as fundamental, more fundamental than his conscious perceptions.

So, for Havel, what is Being? Havel uses a number of terms as synonyms: *order of Being, mystery of Being, order of existence, the hidden sphere, absolute horizon, final horizon*.[6] The final two terms are significant because they point back to the existence of other horizons, two in fact, as we shall see.[7] But *Being* is by far the most common term. Havel gives countless, basically consistent definitions and descriptions of Being. The one following here is from his most formal presentation of his world-view, in the final sixteen letters to Olga:

> The experience of Being [is] . . . the experience that something is. At the very least, there is I, the one having the experience, there is the experience as such, and there is, and must be, intrinsically something that I experience; and if I alone existed—which seems highly unlikely, though theoretically, of course not out of the question—and everything else were merely my dream, this would still be true: for even a dream is an experience, an experience of something, and thus it too is a form of Being. (*Letters*, p. 358)

This "experience that something is" has two layers: "The first layer . . . includes all my direct experience of the world and myself as they manifest themselves to me on various levels of perception. The second—far less direct and vivid, yet incomparably more profound and essential—is the experience of Being in the sense that I am using it here" (*Letters*, p. 359).

The first layer of experience, the first horizon, gives one a sense of being some*where* and some*thing*, but it does not exhaust the content of the experience. There is a further, absolute horizon, a second layer, an experience of "something beyond which there are no more 'beyonds' and beyond which there is, therefore, nothing to be, because this is the 'last of everything,' of every entity" (*Letters*, p. 359).

> Being . . . is not, therefore, simply a kind of nail on which everything hangs, but is itself the absoluteness of all "hanging"; it is the essence of the existence of everything that exists; it is what joins everything that exists together, its order and its memory, its source, its will and its aim, what holds it "together," as it were, and makes it participatory in its unity, its "uniqueness" and its meaningfulness. (*Letters*, p. 359)

Readers of Havel who are familiar with modern philosophy will see here clear reflections of Heidegger's notions of Being, of *Sein* and *Dasein*. They will also see something of the cramped and crabbed style of the twentieth century's most infamously nearly incomprehensible philosopher.[8] Here we need only note the connection, but not examine it. Havel's prose is difficult to read, but it is, I think, understandable, if not lucid.

Perhaps the simplest summary of Havel's concept of Being is this: Being is that which lies at the most basic level of reality; it is not just the content of one's perception, and it is not just phenomena. Being is the *isness* of all that is.

This definition may seem rather slim pickings for a concept of fundamental reality. The definition looks like a tautology: Being is what is. But for Havel, Being appears to us with a very rich character. Note the phrase *appears to us*, for that phrase carries a load of philosophic baggage.

What we know about Being is what we perceive Being unveiling to us. For Havel it unveils much, first about itself, and then about who and what we are, how we are to live, and what we are to value. In *Letters to Olga* Havel describes four experiences that reveal to him much about Being itself, our human identity and our responsibility in the world of everyday experience. The first experience is mystical or spiritual; the second, a profound case of conscience; the third, an instance of empathy; the fourth, a deep sense of guilt or shame at a significant failure to live in the truth. We will discuss each of these as they relate to Havel's worldview. The first concerns the glorious and unitive nature of Being.

Being: The shimmering tree. Twice in *Letters to Olga* Havel describes and reflects on a sudden, unexpected experience of being drawn out of time into a "moment of supreme bliss, of infinite joy, . . . a moment of supreme self-awareness, a supremely elevating state of the soul, a totally harmonic merging of existence with itself and with the entire world" (*Letters*, p. 221). This occurred while he was in Heřmanice and was looking through the prison fence at the crown of a tree whose leaves "shimmered and trembled slightly."[9] Here is his recollection of this experience:

> As I watched the imperceptible trembling of its leaves against an endless sky, I was overcome by a sensation that is difficult to describe: all at once, I seemed to rise above all the coordinates of my momentary existence in the world into a kind of state outside time in which all the beautiful things I had ever seen and experienced existed in a total "co-present"; I felt a sense of reconciliation, indeed of an almost gentle consent to the inevitable course of things as revealed to me now, and this combined with a carefree determination to face what had to be faced. A profound amazement at the sovereignty of Being became a dizzying sensation of tumbling endlessly into the abyss of its mystery; an unbounded joy at being alive, at having been given

the chance to live through all I have lived through, and at the fact that everything has a deep and obvious meaning—this joy formed a strange alliance in me with a vague horror at the inapprehensibility and unattainability of everything I was so close to in that moment, standing at the very "edge of the finite"; I was flooded with a sense of ultimate happiness and harmony with the world and myself, with that moment, with all the moments I could call up, and with everything invisible that lies behind it and which has meaning. I would even say that I was somehow "struck by love," though I don't know precisely for whom or what. (*Letters*, p. 331)

In this experience, Havel passes beyond the first horizon, the experience of the prison yard, the pile of iron on which he sits, the work he is taking a break from, even the tree itself, the slight breeze and the sun. He is on the brink of the second horizon, the very "edge of the finite," and he experiences it as sovereign, endless, not just benign and beautiful, but worthy of love. Einstein is credited with saying that the most important question is, "Is the universe friendly?" Havel would perhaps respond, "I don't know about the universe, but Being itself is more than friendly."

Being: The voice of conscience. The second experience reveals for Havel the moral nature of Being. Here Havel ponders why, when he boards a streetcar late at night with no conductor to observe him, he always feels guilty when he thinks of not paying the fare. Then he comments about the interior dialogue that ensues:

Who, then, is in fact conversing with me? Obviously someone I hold in higher regard than the transport commission, than my best friends (this would come out when the voice would take issue with their opinions), and higher, in some regards than myself, that is, myself as subject of my existence-in-the-world and the carrier of my "existential" interests (one of which is the rather natural effort to save a crown). Someone who "knows everything" (and is therefore omniscient), is everywhere (and therefore omnipresent) and remembers everything; someone who, though infinitely understanding, is entirely incorruptible; who is for me, the highest and utterly unequivocal authority in all moral questions and who is thus Law itself; someone eternal, who through himself makes me eternal as well, so that I cannot imagine the arrival of a moment when everything will come to an end, thus terminating my dependence on him as well; someone to whom I relate entirely and for whom, ultimately, I would do everything. At the same time, this "someone" addresses me directly and personally (not merely as an anonymous public passenger, as the transport commission does). (*Letters*, pp. 345-46)

These reflections are close, if not identical, to a fully theistic conception of God. Surely some Being that is omniscient, omnipresent and good, and who addresses you directly and personally, must himself (itself just doesn't fit these criteria) be personal. Havel too sees this. And yet he draws back from the conclusion:

> But who is it? God? There are many subtle reasons why I'm reluctant to use that word; one factor here is a certain sense of shame (I don't know exactly for what, why and before whom), but the main thing, I suppose, is a fear that with this all too specific designation (or rather assertion) that "God is," I would be projecting an experience that is entirely personal and vague (never mind how profound and urgent it may be), too single-mindedly "outward," onto that problem-fraught screen called "objective reality," and thus I would go too far beyond it. (*Letters*, p. 346)[10]

So while Being manifests characteristics that seem to demand a commitment to theism, Havel avoids this conclusion by shifting his attention from Being (as an objective existent) to himself (as a reflector on his conscious experience). What Havel does draw from this experience—to very good advantage, by the way—is that Being has a moral dimension. Being, then, is the "good" ontological foundation for human moral responsibility, both on an individual level as users of the transport system and on a public level as politicians. We will return to this theme when we deal with the sixth worldview question (How can a person distinguish between right and wrong?).[11] We turn now to consider the second worldview question: What is the nature of the external world?

The Universe Around Us

Though Havel once worked in a science laboratory, he is not much interested in what we can learn about the world from science and technology. He appears to accept the general scientific explanations of the workings of the universe, the complex interplay of matter and energy. But the universe is more than brute matter. In cosmology Havel is impressed with the anthropic cosmological principle and the case that it makes for the intentionality of the emergence of the universe and of us as personal beings within the universe. And he notes as well as the Gaia hypothesis, the theory that the elements of the universe are so interwoven and interdependent that they form a single system, a sort of "megaorganism" (*Art,* pp. 170-71).[12] The anthropic cosmological principle has some merit as a scientific theory; the Gaia hypothesis, even in its most scientific form, is not granted much credibility in scientific circles.[13] But neither hard science nor these speculative theories merits much of Havel's attention.

Rather, what is significant for Havel about the external universe in its physical aspects is its appearance as part of the immediate horizon of human consciousness. It is the first thing we perceive when we begin to perceive. It is the external universe in its various manifestations that can mislead us into thinking that we are only it. Actually we are in our fundamental nature both in this universe and out of it, as we shall see in Havel's answer to the third worldview question: What is a human being?

The Emergent Self

Havel again confronts us with the language of phenomenology and existentialism. He does not give the relatively easy-to-understand answers that, say, a typical naturalist would give: a human being is a highly complex machine whose mystery is the only complexity we do not yet understand. Nor does he give a fully theistic answer: a human being is a person created in the image of God. His approach is rather from the inside out: he asks, What is it that human beings perceive themselves to be?

One short answer hides in its cleverness a quite complex notion: "Man is both the question and the questioner" (*Letters,* p. 226). When human beings come to consciousness, they wonder who they are. They ask questions. They find themselves both at one with and apart from what they experience. It is this existence in two worlds that defines who they are: "Man is the only creature who is both a part of Being (and thus a bearer of its mystery), and aware of that mystery as a mystery" (*Letters,* p. 255). Aware of the mystery, yes. In receipt of its explanation, no.

Our perception of our solidarity with and our separateness from Being constitutes our situation in the world. Our "I" is constituted by Being yet stands over against Being. The temptation is to sink into the immediate horizon of our consciousness, that is, to sink into the world, getting our identity from our proximity and likeness to things. The temptation is especially strong in a technological world which entices by the luring prospect but the false hope of satisfying all our desires by machinery: A human being "is an alien in the world because he is still somehow bound up in Being, and he is alienated from Being because he has been thrown into the world" (*Letters*, p. 321).

Havel calls this alienation *thrownness*, an odd Heideggerian term but one we must understand if we are to grasp Havel's concept of being human. Of course, all of this heady terminology seems abstract, divorced from our experience, speculative and, so far, without a shred of evidence that what is being said is true. But Havel, unlike some of his philosophic compeers, explains what this all means in terms of experience. This brings us to the third of Havel's paradigmatic experiences.

Thrownness, empathy and the significant other. To give a concrete illustration of thrownness, the ordinary human alienation of the self, Havel recounts an experience that he once had while watching television:

> Several days ago, during the weather report . . . something went wrong in the studio and the sound cut out, though the picture continued as usual (there was neither the announcement "Do not adjust your sets" nor landscape photographs, as there usually is in such cases). The employee of the Meteorological Institute who was explaining the forecast quickly grasped what had happened, but because she was not a professional announcer, she didn't know what to do. At this point a strange thing happened: the mantle of routine fell away and before us there suddenly stood a confused, unhappy and terribly embarrassed woman: she stopped talking, looked in desperation at us, then somewhere off to the side, but there was no help from that direction. She could scarcely hold back her tears. (*Letters*, p. 321-22)

Havel immediately reflects on what he sees:

> Exposed to the view of millions, yet desperately alone, thrown into an unfamiliar, unexpected and unresolvable situation, incapable of conveying through mime that she was above it all (by shrugging her shoulders and smiling, for instance), drowning in embarrassment, she stood there in all the primordial nakedness of human helplessness, face-to-face with the big bad world and herself, with the absurdity of her position, and the desperate question of what to do with herself, how to rescue her dignity, how to acquit herself, how to be. Exaggerated as it may seem, I suddenly saw in that event

an image of the primal situation of humanity: a situation of separation, of being cast into an alien world and standing there before the question of self. (*Letters*, p. 322)

But this experience of alienation is not limited to the weather forecaster. Havel suddenly recognizes his own "thrownness."

Moreover, I realized at once that with the woman, I was experiencing— briefly—an almost physical dread; with her, I was overwhelmed by a terrible sense of embarrassment; I blushed and felt her shame; I too felt like crying. Irrespective of my will, I was flooded with an absurdly powerful compassion for this stranger (a surprising thing here, of all places, where in spite of yourself you share the general tendency of the prisoners to see everything related to television as a part of the hostile world that locked them up): I felt miserable because I had no way of helping her, of taking her place, or at least of stroking her hair. (*Letters*, p. 322)

The sense of being alone, without the support of any system in or out of this world: this is the plight of people who begin to grasp just what they are in the world. This is the plight, but then there are the possibilities, the potentials for the future. Though human beings are separated from Being, "thrown" into the world, they are not captured by the world unless they succumb:

Human personality is . . . a large set of possibilities, potentials, perspectives, relationships, demands, opinions, and anticipated responses; it is something open, always actual; not merely a phenomenon, but a source of thinkable phenomena as well; not merely a concrete lived life, but a way of life itself and a living alternative, something that speaks to us and provokes us again and again. (*Letters*, p. 138)

What then should we do with our openness, our freedom? For Havel it is clear: we should return to Being, to sense behind the immediate horizon the ultimate horizon from which we have been thrown. And how do we begin to do that? By responding to the cries of people like the weather forecaster and by taking responsibility not only for our actions but for those of others, in fact "for everything," thus re-rooting our lives in the ground from which we came (*Letters*, p. 324).

For Havel, "the secret of man is the secret of his responsibility" (*Letters*, p. 311). A person's very identity is tied to responsibility: "We find ourselves in a state of responsibility before having decided for it, before we could choose to be responsible at all" (*Letters*, p. 312).[14] And to whom are we responsible? Being, of course, Being that is conscious to us via our conscience, Being that is infinite, omniscient, incorruptibly moral and seemingly personal. In acting responsibly we then make ourselves to be who it is we become. In this we hear the echoes of Sartre's "existence precedes essence." But we hear it with a decidedly non-Sartrean twist. For Sartre, any decision entered into with eyes wide opened and with passionate commitment constitutes not just authentic existence but the good for you. For Havel, Being is intrinsically good; one's responsibility is to move within the framework of this goodness. Havel doesn't use the word *good* with relation to Being, but his notion of responsibility clearly demands it.

Notice that in discussing Havel's answer to "What is a human being?" we have necessarily begun to discuss his answer to worldview question six (How can a person distinguish between right and wrong?). This should suggest that Havel is being unnecessarily humble in saying that he is not a philosopher and does not have a systematic worldview. In any case, we now turn our attention to worldview question four: What happens to a person at death?

Death: Life in the Memory of Being

It may take an act of faith to believe in the resurrection of the body, as do traditional Christians, or reincarnation, as do Hindus. But the mental images that accompany the concepts lend substance to these notions. It is far more difficult to imagine, say, the immortality of the soul. But that is the view that Havel takes. "Human existence," he says, "not only extends beyond the physical existence of its bearer, it clearly goes even beyond the physical existence of the experience of it by others. . . . Human existence . . . will endure, once and for all, in the 'memory of Being' " (*Letters*, p. 139; cf. p. 155). Does this mean that an individual soul will be permanently self-conscious or will continue to be an agent? Havel doesn't say.[15] But life after death will be more than Abraham Lincoln's goodness living on after him.

Havel counsels Olga not to think too much about death, but he also insists that death is part of what makes life meaningful: "I think that con-sciousness is a devilishly influential 'element of the organism' and that our 'desire to live' does not derive at all from our ability to put death out of our minds, but quite the contrary: the awareness of death is the most essential starting point for any genuinely human, i.e., conscious and deliberate, will to life" (Letters, pp. 239-40). We learn to transcend death, he says, "by virtue of an existential metaexperience of the 'absolute hori-zon' " (Letters, p. 240). Here, I presume, Havel means an experience like that of the shimmering tree in Heřmanice. Lifted out of time, Havel was reunited with the Being from which he was "thrown," this time without losing consciousness of his separate self.

Havel's thoughts on death undoubtedly became more intimately per-sonal after his accidental bout with death. In September 1989, just months before he would become president, during a rowdy party with lit-erary friends at a country retreat, Havel, drunk as a skunk as we used to say in Nebraska, stumbled into a mill pond and almost drowned. Barely saved from the ice-cold water, he soon after contracted pneumonia, which for him has been a recurrent problem.[16] John Keane, who tells this story, believes that the "episode had an immediate sobering effect on him."[17] Though one does not find in Havel's works many references to what happens after death, Havel continues to have more than a passing interest in the subject. In 1996 Havel was questioned by a television interviewer about his introduction to a Czech translation of The Tibetan Book of the Dead. Havel said:

> We know about death. We know that we all die, and this [knowledge] dis-tinguishes us from other beings. . . . The individual must first of all think about if and why s/he either acts only within a given time on earth or tries to behave, as Masaryk said, sub species aeternitatis, that is, reckon upon eter-nity when acting, as if everything is being recorded and evaluated, and as if each one of our actions may or may not be an event that can for ever change the universe.[18]

It is unclear what impact the Tibetan Book of the Dead had on Havel's notion of the survival of the human spirit as part of the memory of Being.

We must now raise the fifth worldview question: How can Havel or anyone else come to know the sorts of things he and all of us believe? That is, how can anyone know anything at all?

Knowing That We Know

Havel never takes on the question of epistemology directly. This is characteristic of phenomenological methodology. As a subject one does not know an object. Rather one focuses attention on the phenomena, that is, the data that are presented to one's consciousness. The object that appears to be the source of one's perception is bracketed out. As Roger Scruton describes it, "All reference to what is susceptible to doubt or mediated by reflection must be excluded from the description of every mental state, leaving the remnant of pure immediacy alone."[19]

But, of course, the phenomena presented to the mind point away from themselves to what they appear to represent. So in actuality no one acts as if the world ended with our perceptions. We act as if there were a reality outside ourselves that comports with these perceptions. If I am presented with phenomena that point to a bus coming at me as I stand in the road, I immediately conclude without any philosophic reflection that a bus is coming at me, and I get out of the way.

But such a philosophy does allow one to reflect on phenomena, to doubt that an object exists as their source and even to conclude that no such object exists outside one's mind. This is what we have seen Havel do with his experience of Being when he feels morally constrained to pay for his tram ride late at night. He is appeared to by something that is infinite, omniscient, incorruptibly moral and seemingly personal. He concludes that it is Being, that this Being is infinite, omniscient and—especially—moral, but he refuses to conclude that this Being is personal, giving one important reason: that such a conclusion may project too much of the inner subjective onto the outer objective. Elsewhere Havel says that the experience of an "absolute horizon" is an "experience of something supremely spiritual." Again he rejects the conclusion that Being is personal, this time citing several unpalatable characteristics of a personal God (*Letters*, p. 233). Do these reasons stand to reason? We will examine them in chapter five. In any case, the sticking point for Havel is the personhood of God. That seems to Havel too much with which to credit Being.

Phenomenology, at least as Havel presents it, does not allow much philosophic certitude about what one claims to know. For Havel, however, there is no hesitation. He is certain and he is adamant: There is Being; Being is a moral arbiter; we are thrown into separate consciousness; we are responsible for our response to our thrownness. Havel is so certain of this that in speech after speech he calls politicians and all of us to be responsible for our actions, even responsible for everything. Take his remarks in a speech in February 1990 to a joint session of the House and Senate in Washington: "The only genuine backbone of all our actions—if they are to be moral—is responsibility. Responsibility to something higher than my family, my country, my company, my success. Responsibility to the order of Being, where all our actions are indelibly recorded and where, and only where, they will be properly judged" (*Art*, p. 19).

Or consider his address to the Polish *Sejm* and Senate a month earlier:

> My presidential program is, therefore, to bring spirituality, moral responsibility, humaneness, and humility into politics and, in that respect, to make clear that there is something above us, that our deeds do not disappear into the black hole of time but are recorded somewhere and are judged, that we have neither the right nor a reason to think that we understand everything and that we can do everything.[20]

Similar comments appear regularly in Havel's public lectures and pronouncements.[21] In a speech at the Vatican in 1999, for example, he quotes the ringing words of Czech Reformer John Hus: "Therefore, faithful Christian, seek Truth, listen to the Truth, hear Truth, love Truth, speak Truth, uphold Truth, defend Truth until death; for Truth shall deliver you from sin, from the Devil, from death of the soul, and, in the end, from death everlasting."[22]

There is in Havel that same tenacious spirit: Knowing the truth leads inevitably toward living in the truth. In recognizing this we have already made substantial progress toward understanding Havel's answer to the sixth worldview question: How can a person distinguish between right and wrong?

Responsibility: Living in the Truth

The foundation for the difference between right and wrong is to be found in Being itself. A person's conscience, if it is rooted in Being, gives access to how one should act. Conscience is, so to speak, "the voice of Being." It can be corrupted; it can be put aside; it can be ignored; but it is always capable of being restored. We are free to follow it or not. When we do follow our conscience, we are, in a phrase Havel uses over and over, *living in the truth*.

In chapter two, I described this concept as follows. Living in the truth involves four main subconcepts: (1) that truth is ontological (there is a truth to live in), (2) that this truth is epistemological (a statement of the way things are), (3) that this truth is ethical (it is the way things should be: one should act as one believes one should act) and (4) that this truth requires a lifelong and total commitment without prevarication or withdrawal. Here I will try to unpack and illustrate these four notions as Havel understands them.

First, there is a truth to live in. In Havel's work that truth is the presence of Being itself—that which makes everything to be. In practice it means that when one is doing what one ought to do, one is expressing the character of Being in the actions of its "thrown," derivative other—that is, in human being. Being, so understood, is a given, a fundamental, a presupposition.

Second, this truth is epistemological. Here we run into a problem. In phenomenology, as I have already pointed out, one does not expect to "know" the world. One can recognize only phenomena as they are perceived; one can know only the contents of one's consciousness. But the acceptance of this notion requires something that is not in the content of one's consciousness. It requires one to "know" or "believe" or "assume" that phenomenology—the notion that we know only our own perceptions—is true. But according to the principles of phenomenology, this can't be known. Phenomenology requires a prior commitment to the truth of its major notion. Call it an act of faith or a pretheoretical commitment, a presupposition or simply a foolish and systematic internal inconsistency, it is the commitment we see Havel making throughout his works.

I think the most charitable interpretation to make is that Václav Havel lives as if he—and all other people of good will—could really know the difference between right and wrong, that this difference is due not to language, culture, time or space, but to fundamental absolutes rooted in reality. He explains why this difference exists: it exists because Being is fundamentally good (though he does not say this directly, it is implied by the fact that we are responsible to Being). But he understands human beings as having been "thrown" from Being in such a fashion that they must become the arbiters of what Being is solely on the basis of phenomena—phenomena perceived via the two horizons, (1) the external world and the inner world of existential consciousness, and (2) the absolute horizon of Being itself. When Being unveils itself as it did for Havel seeing the shimmering tree in Heřmanice, riding on the night tram and watching the sound go dead in the TV studio, it does so with such noetic power that doubt about the objectivity of a reality outside his mind is eliminated. So is doubt about the moral character of Being and the sense of responsibility that we all have.

But Being does not give us such "existential metaexperiences" very often. Thus the doubt, the shame of objectifying one's imagination, the uncertainty of much of life. Indeed, Havel himself confesses frequently to feelings of inadequacy. Sometimes for Havel these guilt feelings themselves provide an experience of Being—or, better, a sense of the absence of Being.

So for Havel in this instance, truth becomes not knowledge of reality, but sincerity or integrity. Living in truth means living as you perceive you should live. It means doing what you believe or think to be right. Truth itself, Havel says, is more than information: "It is information avouched by a human being with his or her whole existence."[23] Anything less is living in a lie. In other words: (3) truth is ethical.

Finally, (4) living in truth requires a lifelong and total commitment without prevarication or withdrawal. Havel frequently holds up Tomáš Garrigue Masaryk, the first president of an independent Czechoslovakia, as exemplary: "What Masaryk taught, he did; and what he did, he taught. The absolute unity of words and deeds, exemplified in his life, undoubtedly deserves our recognition and admiration."[24] Havel too shines in this regard, though he fears he does not. And that brings us to the fourth key paradigmatic experience Havel repeatedly mentions in his work. It is so central to an understanding of Havel that though we have looked at it before, we must examine it again.

A failure to live in the truth. As we have noted, in 1977, during his first imprisonment, Havel wrote a request for release, cleverly wording it so that he could provide to the public prosecutor what would be needed for his release while adhering to what he believed was, strictly speaking, true. Havel was released, and the authorities broadcast a twisted form of his request and made it look as though he had betrayed the cause for which he was arrested. This had a profound effect on the subsequent course of his life.

Havel, always one to reflect and self-reflect, felt that he had indeed betrayed not just the cause and himself but also the very being of all Being. To atone for this he spoke even more freely, and thus openly courted rearrest. It was not long in coming. But while the damage to Havel's reputation was mended, the damage to his psyche has, I think, never been fully healed. He has continued to reflect on this incident, making it one of a half-dozen or so most significant events that shape both his public and private life.[25]

Living in the truth would have required him to consider the broadest of contexts whenever he spoke of significant matters. He expresses this principle in the final sixteen letters to Olga: "The truth lies not only in what is said, but also in who says it, and to whom, why, and how and under what circumstances it is expressed" (*Letters*, p. 347).

It is a truth that has been won by failure and by profound self-berating reflection in which he makes, as he says, a "desperate attempt to hide from myself the hard fact that the failure was mine," a failure of the "I of my I" (*Letters*, p. 350). As Havel contemplates his failure five years after the fact, he seems to have come to terms with it. He sees it as "some kind of rescue operation mounted by fate." Being was unveiling to him an insight into moral reality that he would not have otherwise understood, let alone internalized:

> I've only now begun to fully realize that the experience wasn't just—from my point of view, at least—an incomprehensible lapse that caused me a lot of pointless suffering; it had a deeply positive and purgative significance, for which I ought to thank my fate instead of cursing it. It thrust me into a drastic but, for that very reason, crucial confrontation with myself; it shook, as it were, my entire "I," "shook out of it" a deeper insight into itself, a more seri-

ous acceptance and understanding of my situation, of my thrownness and my horizons, and led me, ultimately, to a new and more coherent consideration of the problem of human responsibility. (*Letters*, p. 342)

Havel goes deeper yet:

For it is only by assuming full responsibility here for one's own elsewhere, only by assuming full responsibility today for one's own yesterday, only by this unqualified assumption of responsibility by the "I" for itself and everything it ever was and did, does the "I" achieve continuity and thus identity with the self. (*Letters*, p. 350)

We may become discouraged, then, when Fistula accuses Foustka of tricking himself by means of the Smichovsky Compensation Syndrome—a syndrome in which Foustka the betrayer sees his betrayal as a "purifying lesson" (*Temptation*, pp. 61-62). Is Havel ripping the scar from his wound? Or is he just being a good dramatist? Or has he combined dramaturgy with self-psychotherapy, seeing the dark side of betrayal and its lessons and trying to sublimate, maybe even suffocate, them in dramatic irony?

One thing we can be sure of: Havel makes more than a fetish of responsibility and living in the truth.

The greengrocer: A case in point. In his long and profound essay "The Power of the Powerless," Havel illustrates the title theme with the story of a greengrocer. Imagine, he says, a greengrocer who places among the onions and carrots a placard with the slogan "Workers of the world, unite!" The placard has come with his vegetables and he is expected to display it. He doesn't give it a thought; it does not express his own views, and he really can't imagine what it might mean. But this is the sort of thing he and his fellow merchants have been doing for years. To refuse could bring trouble from the ubiquitous secret police.

What does his putting the sign in the window really mean? Not that the grocer has any real belief that the workers of the world should unite (to that he is indifferent). It does mean, however, that he is submitting to the order imposed on him by the reigning ideology. The message is subliminal but definite: "Verbally, it might be expressed this way: 'I, the greengrocer XY, live here and I know what I must do. I behave in the manner expected of me. I can be depended upon and am beyond reproach. I am obedient and therefore I have the right to be left in peace' " (*Living*, p. 42). The message is addressed both to those above him and to those alongside him who may be acting as informers. It says, "It's okay to leave me alone. I won't rock the boat."

> The sign helps the greengrocer to conceal from himself the low foundations of his obedience, at the same time concealing the low foundations of power. It hides behind the facade of something high. And that something is *ideology.*
>
> Ideology is a specious way of relating to the world. It offers human beings the illusion of an identity, of dignity, and of morality while making it easier for them to *part* with them. . . . It is a veil behind which human beings can hide their own "fallen existence," their trivialization, and their adaptation to the status quo. (*Living*, pp. 41-42)

Havel then imagines what would happen if one day the grocer decided not to display the sign, what if he stopped voting in the farcical elections, started saying "what he really thinks at political meetings" and began to show "solidarity with those whom his conscience commands him to support"? Havel says, "In this revolt the greengrocer steps out of living within the lie. He rejects the ritual and breaks the rules of the game. He discovers once more his suppressed identity and dignity. He gives his freedom a concrete significance. His revolt is an attempt to *live within the truth*" (*Living*, p. 55).

What then happens to the grocer?

> The bill is not long in coming. He will be relieved of his post as manager of the shop and transferred to the warehouse. His pay will be reduced. His hopes for a holiday in Bulgaria will evaporate. His children's access to higher education will be threatened. His superiors will harass him and his fellow workers will wonder about him. . . . Thus the power structure, through the agency of those who carry out the sanctions, those anonymous components of the system, will spew the greengrocer from its mouth. The system, through its alienating presence in people, will punish him for his rebellion. (*Living*, p. 55)

What will happen to the system?

> By breaking the rules of the game, he has disrupted the game as such. He has exposed it as a mere game. He has shattered the world of appearances,

the fundamental pillar of the system. He has upset the power structure by tearing apart what holds it together. He has demonstrated that living a lie is living a lie. . . . He has shown everyone that it *is* possible to live within the truth. (*Living,* p. 56)

We must not think that living in the truth is dangerous only in a totalitarian (or, as Havel calls Czechoslovakia before the Velvet Revolution, a post-totalitarian) society.[26] Were Havel to speak about, say, American society at the end of the 1990s, he would focus on the ideologies of consumerism and schlock TV entertainment, among a host of other matters. Living in the truth would mean not purchasing the most convenient appliances, the largest house, the latest and most luxurious car, and the most advanced entertainment system. That too would have a cost: the family that did so would be looked down on by the neighbors, and the children would have to explain their odd behavior to their friends and sneak off to the neighbor's house to watch violent television shows and listen to obscene rap music. It would not be difficult to multiply illustrations.

Virtues and vices. There is nothing unusual in the vices Havel rejects and the virtues he affirms. Among the vices he lists apathy, conformity, routine performance, "egotism, hypocrisy, indifference, cowardice, fear, resignation and the desire to escape every personal responsibility, regardless of the general consequences"; likewise, "the power of ideologies, systems, apparat, bureaucracy, artificial languages and political slogans" (*Living,* pp. 13, 35 153). These characterize the post-totalitarian world of Czechoslovakia. Havel writes, "A world where 'truth' flourishes not in a dialectic climate of genuine knowledge, but in a climate of power motives, is a world of mental sterility, petrified dogmas, rigid and unchangeable creeds leading inevitably to creedless despotism (*Living,* p. 16). When he addressed the Czechoslovak people in his first speech as president, Havel said: "Our main enemy today is our own bad traits: indifference to the common good; vanity; personal ambition; and rivalry" (*Open,* p. 395). Perhaps the capstone of vices is hatred, a vice he directly analyzed and countered at an Oslo Conference on "The Anatomy of Hate" (*Art,* p. 19).

Among the virtues Havel lists selflessness, "trust, openness, responsibility, solidarity, love," justice, honor, friendship, fidelity, courage, empathy, patience and the willingness to sacrifice for these virtues.[27] All of these are, of course, topped off by the virtue of living in the truth. In a speech before the European Parliament, Havel lists a host of public virtues that he labels European values:

> respect for the unique human being, and for humanity's freedoms, rights and dignity; the principle of solidarity; the rule of law and equality before the law; the protection of minorities of all types; democratic institutions; the separation of legislative, executive and judicial powers; a pluralist political system; respect for private ownership and private enterprise, and market economy; and a furtherance of civil society.[28]

The more social and political of these values, I suspect, Havel would recognize, have historical origins. But certainly the more generic of these virtues and vices are rooted in the ordinary conscience of ordinary people. He opens his essay "Politics and Conscience" with a description of the basic orientation that he as a young boy and peasants have in common.

> Both the boy and the peasant are far more intensely rooted in what some philosophers call "the natural world," or *Lebenswelt*, than most modern adults. They have not yet grown alienated from the world of their actual personal experience, the world which has its morning and evening, its *down* (the earth) and its *up* (the heavens), where the sun rises daily in the east, traverses the sky and sets in the west, and where concepts like "at home" and "in foreign parts", good and evil, beauty and ugliness, near and far, duty and work, still mean something living and definite. . . .
>
> At the basis of this world are values which are simply there, perennially, before we ever speak of them, before we reflect upon them and inquire about them. It owes its internal coherence to something like a "pre-speculative" assumption that the world functions and is generally possible at all only because there is something beyond its horizon, something beyond or above it that might escape our understanding and grasp but, for just that reason, firmly grounds this world, bestows upon it its order and measure and is the hidden source of all the rules, customs, commandments, prohibitions and norms that hold within it. (*Living*, pp. 135-36)

Havel is convinced as well that the fundamental values are common to all major religions. If their adherents were to emphasize what they have in common, these various traditions could maintain their distinctives in a pluralistic global society but recognize their source in something transcendent beyond all of them. Reconciliation would result.[29]

Boy, peasant, religious adherent and sophisticated intellectual, in the final analysis, get their ethical orientation from Being.[30] In perhaps his clearest expression of this, Havel says, "Being—as the absolute horizon of our relating—is for us— as a 'voice' and a 'cry'—identical with a moral order (as though Being were not only the 'reasoning mind' of everything that exists, but its 'heart' as well)" (*Letters*, p. 374).

Being does indeed cry out to Havel, and never more so than when it cries out about the destructive impact of modern technology: "The chimney 'soiling the heavens' is not just a technologically corrigible flaw of design, or a tax paid for better consumers tomorrow, but a symbol of a civilization which has renounced the absolute, which ignores the natural world and disdains its imperatives" (*Living*, p. 138).

Writing in 1978 he said that IBM is even worse than the Czechoslovakian Skoda:

> Whereas Skoda merely grinds out the occasional obsolete nuclear reactor to meet the needs of backward COMECON members IBM is flooding the world with even more advanced computers, while its employees have no influence over what their product does to the human soul and to human society. They have no say in whether it enslaves or liberates mankind, whether it will save us from the apocalypse or simply bring the apocalypse closer. (*Disturbing*, p. 14)

Any solution to our ecological crisis—if indeed there is a solution—will have to involve a recognition "that we are not the masters of Being, but only a part of Being" (*Art*, p. 79). Much more could be said about Havel's critique of technology, a critique that reflects much of Heidegger's analysis. In any case, it is not technology as such that will help solve the problems the Czech Republic or any other nation faces today.

So to what end is society moving? Or is it moving to any end? Does history have a *telos*? The seventh worldview question (What, if anything, is the meaning of our human sojourn on earth?) focuses on this issue.

Telos: The End of the Matter

Some worldviews address the meaning or designed direction of human history largely in the negative, even the tragic negative. "History is bunk," Henry Ford is quoted as saying. "Pay no attention to the man behind the curtain," said the Wizard of Oz. "Look in amazement and wonder or grief and terror at what is in front of you; that's all there is." That's nihilism. "That's all there is now, but you can make something of the future by your own intentions. Just don't look for any meaning or significance that transcends the immediate horizon. There is no absolute horizon." That's humanism or atheistic existentialism.

Some worldviews are more optimistic. Christians, for example, hold that God is ultimately in charge: the kingdom of God is coming, if not in material form, at least in a world that transcends this one. History is the concrete realization of God's intentions for his creation.

Havel rejects the notion of a coming transcendent kingdom brought about by a personal deity, and he is highly dubious of any hope for a material utopia. Attempts to bring about such a utopia will end, if not begin, in violence and injustice, because they rest on unrealistic ideologies. Ideologies first envision utopias; then they either manipulate the populace into thinking utopia already exists—as it actually does for the elite—or they attempt to realize it by oppressive force, justifying their actions with such clichés as "To make an omelet you have to crack a few eggs." More than eggs are cracked; heads roll.

But Havel is not without hope for the future. His hope rests at least in part on his understanding of who we are as human beings. We are self-conscious beings *thrown out* from Being. And as we are *thrown out* as self-conscious beings, the world as well is *thrown out* as unselfconscious being: "Man and the world come into being at the same time, as two 'dimensions' of a single act of separation. . . . When the 'I' is constituted, the world is constituted along with it" (*Letters*, p. 373).

But we are at the same time also *thrown into Being*. We lose our unity with our source, but we acquire a longing for it and thus know intuitively that we are more than impersonal beings, more than cogs in the machinery of the world. The meaning of history is tied up with our living in light of these two poles of our existence—Being and the world.

To make his view clearer, Havel tells the story of human history by redefining key terms of Christian theology. The Edenic paradise is a " 'rec-

ollection' of a lost participation in the integrity of Being"; the Fall is the
act of "separation" that takes place when we gain "knowledge of the
self"; the last judgment is our "confrontation with the absolute horizon";
salvation is "supreme transcendence, that 'quasi-identification' with the
fullness of Being, to which humanity is constantly aspiring." The fact that
all attempts at utopias end in disaster indicates that "the kingdom of God
is not 'of this earth' " (*Letters*, p. 375).

He ends his explanation with an eloquent recasting of biblical escha-
tology:

> Yes: man is in fact nailed down—like Christ on the cross—to a grid of para-
> doxes: stretched between the horizontal world and the vertical of Being;
> dragged down by the hopelessness of existing-in-the-world on the one
> hand, and the unattainability of the absolute on the other, he balances
> between the torment of not knowing his mission and the joy of carrying it
> out, between nothingness and meaningfulness. And like Christ, he is in fact
> victorious, by virtue of his defeats; through perceiving absurdity, he once
> again finds meaning; through personal failure, he once more discovers
> responsibility; through the defeat of several prison sentences, he gains a vic-
> tory—at the very least—over himself (as an object of worldly temptations);
> and through death—his last and greatest defeat—he finally triumphs over
> his fragmentation; by completing, for all time, his outline in the "memory of
> Being," he returns at last—having rejected nothing of his "otherness"—to
> the womb of integral Being. (*Letters*, p. 375)

If the end, the *telos,* of each person is to complete "for all time his outline
in the memory of Being," then one may infer that the meaning of history
is the collected, unified meanings of every life as each life completes its
outline. History does have meaning: the meanings that each life contrib-
utes to the memory of Being. Havel sees all of this in the terms of his own
life and death.

We may wish to raise again the issue of the fourth worldview question:
How does Havel know any of this is true? Atheistic existentialists and
humanists rely on science and rational thought; Christians and Muslims
defer to revelation from God himself. Havel looks elsewhere—to the
unveiling of Being mediated by existential metaexperiences. It is from
these experiences that Havel derives what can only be seen—in light of
the grim history of his own life in and out of prison—as a foundational

faith. Perhaps one should call it hope. Havel has a lot to say about that.

Hope for the Future

No one can rightfully accuse Havel of misty-eyed optimism. His experience of the immediate horizon of prison life and the agonies of people around the world and of his own nation in particular: these have removed all naiveté. Havel's plays plumb the depths of political and social absurdity. Only when one fully recognizes and participates in the reality of modern life can genuine hope emerge: "There are times when we must sink to the bottom of our misery to understand truth, just as we must descend to the bottom of a well to see the stars in broad daylight" (*Living*, p. 89).

Surely there is in Havel's life enough sinking "to the bottom of misery." The present is grim, Havel sees from his prison cell and even later as he experiences the reality of practical politics, but he remains hopeful. We need to "come to our senses"; there must be an "existential revolution, . . . a kind of general mobilization of human consciousness, of the human mind and spirit, human responsibility, human reason" (*Summer*, p. 116).

Havel speaks little about the details of what he has in mind, and I think it is also fair to say that he doesn't see much realization of what he hopes for. But still he calls for a radical transformation. And still he is hopeful.

Hope, however, is not won by observation of the immediate horizon; it is not simple optimism, nor is it predicated on prognostication. Hope comes only by penetrating to the ultimate horizon of Being.

> Either we have hope in us or we don't; it is a dimension of the soul, and it's not essentially dependent on some particular observation of the world or estimate of the situation. Hope is not prognostication. It is an orientation of the spirit, an orientation of the heart; it transcends the world that is immediately experienced, and is anchored somewhere beyond its horizons. (*Disturbing*, p. 181)[31]

In his lecture at the Future of Hope conference in Hiroshima in 1995, Havel expanded this notion:

> The primary origin of hope is, to put it simply, metaphysical. By that I mean to say that hope is more, and goes deeper, than a mere optimistic inclination or disposition of the human mind, determined genetically, biologically,

chemically, culturally, or otherwise. . . . Somewhere behind all that, acknowledged or unacknowledged, and articulated in different ways, but always most profound, is humanity's experience with its own Being and with the Being of the world. This profound hope, in its very essence reaches beyond death. (*Art*, p. 239-40)

Those who are counting on technology to save civilization may come to despair. "But those who believe, in all modesty, in the mysterious power of their own human Being, which mediates between them and the mysterious power of the world's Being, have no reason to despair at all" (*Art*, p. 94).

In "Faith in the World," a mistitled essay in *Civilization*, Havel, I think, indicates more explicitly than usual that the foundation for his hope is fundamentally religious and may require explicitly religious expression. Religions are clearly different, he argues, but what they hold in common is more important than what distinguishes one from another.

Perhaps the way out of the current bleak situation could be found in the search for what unites the various religions and cultures, in the search for common sources, principles, certitudes, aspirations and imperatives, a purpose-minded search; and then, applying means adequate to the needs of our time, we could cultivate all matters of human coexistence and endeavor, and at the same time the planet on which it is our destiny to live, suffusing it with all the spirit of what I would call the common spiritual and moral minimum.[32]

Then, realizing that this is a tall order, Havel asks whether "charismatic prophets or modern messiahs or even some kind of historical miracle" might be necessary to accomplish the "existential revolution" that is required. It would not be difficult to answer yes to that.

Havel's own actions in the past ten years of his direct political engagement are a testimony to his living not just in truth but in hope. Discouragement abounds in his self-witness to this feeling, but it never overwhelms a fundamental attitude of hope. His actions and attitudes, Havel believes, will become a part of the memory of Being; he wishes them to be worthy of their place.

4

The Intellectual
as Politician

It is my profound conviction that the world requires today more than ever truly
enlightened and thoughtful politicians who are bold and broad-minded enough to
consider also those things which lie beyond the scope of their immediate influence
in both space and time.

VÁCLAV HAVEL, ADDRESS AT OXFORD UNIVERSITY

VÁCLAV HAVEL—THINKER, WRITER, DRAMATIST, dissident, suddenly the
chief officer of a nation. What kind of politician does this intellectual
make? Is he, as some have speculated, the world's first philosopher-king?
No, not that. Philosopher, maybe, but not king. From the beginning, when
he appeared in public in a sweater instead of a suit, and for more than a
decade, he has attempted to be one of the people, one who has ideas and
takes decided stances on matters of public policy, but who rarely if ever
attempts to manipulate the populace either by stealth or by sheer power.

As intellectual and politician Havel is almost unique, I think, in the
annals of the modern world. With a political philosophy forged in reflection on Martin Heidegger, Edmund Husserl, Jan Patočka and Tomáš Garrigue Masaryk, and in the context of dissident action, he entered the
public square as a leader. His five years in prison and many more years
under the surveillance of the secret police had prepared him for continued challenges, but only partly for the role he has played as president.
The details of Havel's life are only now emerging, in publications like
John Keane's *Václav Havel: A Political Tragedy in Six Acts.*[1] Much more
needs to be done on every phase of Havel's literary and political career.

Though I will not go into detail on Havel's performance as a politician, I do wish to focus on his conception of politics and its relation to the role that intellectuals can and should play. The impetus for this book came from my early interest in Havel as an intellectual, as a man who, however and wherever he has lived, has done so with a minimum of gut-level reaction and a maximum of thought. His early understanding of human responsibility; his concerted effort to live in the truth; his willingness to openly confess when he feels that he has failed, and to move on: all of these make him exemplary. His understanding of intellectuals and their role fits hand in glove with his worldview.

Political Intellectuals in Drama

We had a first look at Havel's understanding of intellectuals when we examined the remarks made by characters in his plays. In *The Memorandum* the intellectual is caricatured as "always hesitant, always full of doubts, too considerate, a dreamer rather than a man of action" (*Memorandum*, p. 68). In *Audience* the Brewmaster sees Vaněk, a writer reduced to the role of a menial brewery worker, as a dissident who sells his principles. Still the intellectual is the one who, though he is kept from employment as a writer by the post-totalitarian system, is more free than his boss. The intellectual lives on principles. The Brewmaster can't afford to do so. In *Largo Desolato*, Leopold, the intellectual, is a writer who is losing a sense of his identity as his inner world collapses; now he is frightened of the secret police and incapable of any in-depth personal relations. "I used to browse around the second-hand bookshops—studying philosophers at my leisure," he says, "spending the nights making notes from their works—taking walks in the park meditating" (*Largo*, p. 52). But no longer; now he is a captive of his own empty soul. In *Temptation*, Foustka, the focal intellectual, is a man who turns against the purely scientific approach of his colleagues to dabble in the occult, only to find that he has been outwitted by the scientists. Finally in *Redevelopment or Slum Clearance*, Plekhanov is the intellectual and moral center of the play; favoring people over programs, art over efficiency, he finds it no longer possible to live in the world of social engineering that his field of architecture has become. So he jumps from the tower of the castle, the decayed symbol of past cultural glory.

What are we to make of these various depictions of the intellectual in society? Certainly it is clear that no character in Havel's plays is an embodiment of Havel's ideal intellectual. However, Havel does deal with several themes and issues that such an intellectual must face: (1) the difficulty and the cost of telling the truth in a society that speaks the debased language of ideology, (2) the relationship between responsibility and personal identity, (3) the effect of compromise on psychological health, (4) the temptation and cost of living in a lie and (5) the triviality of a life lived for anything other than the truth. But we look in vain for the intellectual hero to enter the stage as the deus ex machina to save the day. Havel's plays are not tragedies; rather, they are absurd comedies that leave the audience with a sense not that the universe is absurd, but that contemporary society—especially, contemporary Czech post-totalitarian society—is absurd.

So, then, what does Havel understand the proper intellectual to be and do? And what sort of intellectual does Havel imagine himself to be?

The Intellectual as Such

In his essays and lectures Havel frequently speaks about the role of the intellectual in modern society. Sometimes he gives a general definition of an intellectual; at other times he describes an intellectual's role. Perhaps the most generic definition appears in an address he gave in 1995 at Victoria University in New Zealand:

> To me, an intellectual is a person who has devoted his or her life to thinking in general terms about the affairs of this world and the broader context of things. Of course, intellectuals are not the only ones who do this. But they do it—if I may use the word—professionally. That is, their principal occupation is studying, reading, teaching, writing, publishing, addressing the public. Often—though certainly not always—this makes them more receptive to more general issues; often—though certainly not always—it leads them to embrace a broader sense of responsibility for the state of the world and its future. (*Art*, p. 206-07)

Havel then notes that a number of people who fit this definition have actually done more harm than good: "Taking an interest in the world as a whole and feeling an increased sense of responsibility for it, intellectuals are often tempted to try to grasp the world as a whole, to explain it entirely, and to offer universal solutions to its problems" (*Art*, p. 207). This leads to ideology, false consciousness, oppressive social engineering and unjust political regimes. But there are many others who have

> seen things in more global terms, recognized the mysterious nature of globality, and humbly deferred to it. Their increased sense of responsibility for this world has not made such intellectuals identify with an ideology; it has made them identify with humanity, its dignity, and its prospects. These intellectuals build people-to-people solidarity. They foster tolerance, struggle against evil and violence, promote human rights and argue for their indivisibility. In a word, they represent what has been called "the conscience of society." They are not indifferent when people in an unknown country on the other side of the planet are annihilated, or when children starve, nor are they unconcerned about global warming and the prospects of future generations leading an endurable life. They care about the fate of virgin forests in faraway places, about whether or not mankind will soon destroy all its nonrenewable resources, or whether a global dictatorship of advertisement, consumerism, and blood-and-thunder stories on TV will ultimately lead the human race to a state of complete idiocy. (*Art*, p. 208)

Clearly Havel is not content for intellectuals to merely see and comment. Yes, the intellectual is "the guardian and bearer of spiritual qualities" (*Art*, p. 95). Yes, the intellectual is "a Cassandra who tells us what is going on outside the walls of the city" and foresees "various threats, horrors and catastrophes" (*Art*, p. 177). Yes, the intellectual "should constantly disturb, should bear witness to the misery of the world, should be provocative by being independent, should rebel against all hidden and open pressure and manipulations, should be the chief doubter of systems of power and its incantations, should be witness to their mendacity" (*Disturbing*, p. 167). Yes, the intellectual should conduct "a deep analysis of the tangled roots of intolerance in our individual and collective unconscious and consciousness, a merciless examination of all the frustrations of loneliness, personal inadequacy, and loss of metaphysical certainties that is one of the sources of human aggression" (*Art*, p. 185). Yes, the intellectual should throw "a sharp light . . . on the misery of the contemporary soul" (Art, p. 185). But no, the role of the intellectual should not end there.[2]

Intellectuals have an obligation to be engaged in politics in the broadest sense of the term. Because civilization faces so many crises, it is important to look to "the sphere of human consciousness and self-knowledge," to Being itself, and it is intellectuals who are best able to do that. The "very spirit and ethos of politics" must begin to be changed. "That is why I wonder whether genuine intellectuals, philosophers, and poets are not virtually duty-bound to take upon themselves all the risks and requirements that go with it, even though they find them rather strange. Is it not time for intellectuals to try to give politics, as it were, [a] postmodern face?" (Art, p. 100).[3]

In an address that he gave when accepting an honorary degree from Oxford University, Havel suggests several specific tasks intellectuals could well perform. First, they could "consider . . . those things which lie beyond the scope of their immediate influence in both space and time." This would entail their rising above the "horizon of their own power interests" or those of their party and acting instead "in accordance with the fundamental interests of today's humanity." They should "look for the truth of this world without claiming to be its professional owner." Rhetoric in service of the truth is vital:

> The true art of politics is the art to win people's support for a good cause even when the pursuit of that cause may interfere with their particular interests at the moment. . . . A good politician of the future should be able to explain without seeking to seduce; he should humbly look for the truth of this world without claiming to be its professional owner; he should alert people to the good qualities in themselves, including a sense of the values and interests which transcend the personal, without giving himself an air of superiority and imposing anything on his fellow humans; he should not yield to the dictates of public moods or of the mass media, while never hindering a constant scrutiny of his own actions.[4]

For Havel such politics is a high calling that deserves the attention of intellectuals, who are uniquely able to respond to the challenge.[5] He lists Winston Churchill as one such intellectual politician and wonders whether it is possible for there to be another like him. Havel concludes by stating two ways intellectuals can take their political responsibility seriously: (1) they can "accept public office" and (2) they can "constantly hold up a mirror to those in authority." Both roles are political; only one is independent.

Havel is often accused of being a dreamer. But, he replies, dreaming itself may be part of the solution: "Who thinks about future generations? Who is concerned about what people will eat, drink, breathe in 100 years, where they will get energy when there are twice as many people living on the planet as today? Only an idealist, a dreamer, a genuinely spiritual person who, they say, is not modern enough."[6]

However, the dreams of the intellectuals will neither be heard nor seen if politics itself is not significantly transformed toward "a deeper responsibility toward the world." That transformation—in fact, the transformation of the whole of humanity—is what Havel wants to see occur; it is a major object of his hope. Politics should be a way of bringing such hope to reality. If we think that this is impossible, Havel has a word for us: Politics is "the art of the impossible."

The Art of the Impossible: Morality in Practice
In one of his clearest statements of the task of politicians, Havel said, "The main task of the present generation of politicians is . . . to assume their share of the responsibility for the long-range prospects of our world and thus to set an example for the public in whose sight they work. Their responsibility is to think ahead boldly, not to fear the disfavor of the crowd; to imbue their actions with a spiritual dimension. . . . After all, politics is a matter of serving the community, which means that it is morality in practice" (Art, p. 223).

Morality in practice expresses a high ideal indeed for politics. And, as we have seen, Havel is constantly striving to express the highest of ideals at the deepest of levels. Tomáš Garrigue Masaryk, the first president of the democratic Czechoslovakia, which lasted for only twenty years, was also a renowned intellectual. He "based his politics on morality," Havel says, so "let us try in a new time and a new way to restore this concept of politics" (Open, p. 395).

Given this conception of politics it is no wonder that Havel should see politics as "the art of the impossible."

> Let us teach ourselves and others that politics can be not only the art of the possible, especially if this means the art of speculation, calculation, intrigue, secret deals, and pragmatic maneuvering, but that it can even be the art of the impossible, namely, the art of improving ourselves and the world. (*Open*, p. 395)

At no time during his ten years of active involvement in the political arena has Havel either wavered in this commitment or ceased to call politicians around the world to live by its principle. As such he has become the moral conscience of international politics.

The Politics of the Intellectual

Given what we see as we look back over Havel's life, it seems odd that Havel denies that he ever intended or expected to engage in politics. He is a writer, he says, a dramatist, an artist in words. But his friend and fellow dissident writer Ivan Klíma demurs:

> I used to say, half jokingly, that Havel became a dramatist simply because at that time the theater was the only platform from which political opinions could be expressed. Right from the beginning, when I got to know him, Havel was, for me, in the first place a politician, in the second place an essayist of genius, and only lastly a dramatist. I am not ordering the value of his achievements but rather the priority of his interests, personal inclination, and enthusiasm.[7]

In any case, Havel's political role emerged naturally from his commitment as a writer and proponent of the freedom of all the arts. As we have seen, his early plays—*The Garden Party* and *The Memorandum*—display by implication the absurdity of post-totalitarian society and thus are political if not by design at least by default. Certainly the authorities thought them political, for they were banned from performance in Czechoslovakia beginning in August of 1968. They continued to be performed elsewhere in Europe and in North America and were an ongoing thorn in the side of the authorities. So, wittingly or not, Havel the dramatist was performing the second political role that he designates for intellectuals: He was holding up a mirror to the authorities.

Havel became explicitly political in his widely circulated and, to the authorities, infuriating "Letter to Gustáv Husak, General Secretary of the Czechoslovak Communist Party," which he wrote in April 1975. Here he charged Husak with running the state on fear, using "ubiquitous, omnipresent state police, . . . [as a] hideous spider whose invisible web runs right through society" (Living, p. 7). People were being reduced to economic units. For self-preservation alone they were succumbing to "the harsh assault on human integrity" (Living, p. 12). There would follow, he argued, the demoralization of life and a crisis in human identity. A politics that no longer promotes the diversity of cultural life stifles it instead: "The overall question, then, is this: what profound intellectual and moral impotence will the nation suffer tomorrow, following the castration of culture today?" (Living, p. 23).

In September 1976 Havel and six other Czech intellectuals signed a letter to Heinrich Böll supporting the right of pop music groups to perform; then Havel helped organize protests against their persecution by the government.[8] But his most important political action is without a doubt his drafting of Charter 77 with Jan Patočka and Jiří Hájek, which set off the Charter 77 movement.[9] The document implored the Czechoslovak authorities to honor the accord that they had signed in Helsinki granting basic human rights. But because the authorities had no intention of actually honoring those rights, Charter 77 called their bluff. The Charter 77 movement, perhaps the most important of several dissident political movements, was active until it was replaced by Civic Forum, the opposition group that negotiated the establishment of the new government after the Velvet Revolution of November 1989.[10]

Among the many political tracts Havel wrote or contributed to, the most important document is "The Power of the Powerless," written in October 1978, which also circulated samizdat (underground) and had a major influence on dissident movements in Poland.[11] As we discussed in chapter three, in this eloquent essay Havel explains the role dissidents can play in the formation of a civil society. Unhappy with the term dissident because of its unsavory connotation, Havel insists that "a 'dissident' is simply a physicist, a sociologist, a worker, a poet, individuals who are merely doing what they feel they must and, consequently, who find themselves in open conflict with the regime" (*Living,* p. 78). Dissidents start from a positive, not a negative, stance. They are simply trying to live in the truth. If the powerless were to stop acting as if the lie were true and were to begin to live in the truth, the locus of power would shift.

Living in the truth requires massive commitment, but not massive action. Havel reminds his readers that Masaryk established a national program "based on the notion of 'small-scale work.'" This means "responsible work in widely different areas of life but within the existing social order, work that would stimulate national creativity and national self-confidence" (*Living,* pp. 80-81). Havel calls on the artists—musicians, writers, painters, sculptors—to continue to perform, to set up a "second," or parallel, culture alongside the bland anticulture of the post-totalitarians.[12] This would "create the conditions for a more human life." "The point where living within the truth ceases to be a mere negation of living with a lie and becomes articulate in a particular way, is the point at which something is born that might be called the 'independent spiritual, social and political life of society'" (*Living,* p. 85). Havel's dissident vision, therefore, was indeed revolutionary. But if such a rebirth of living in the truth should occur, the revolution would be velvet.

It is no wonder that Havel was considered one of the most dangerous dissidents. Every effort was taken to make his views unavailable, to make them obscure or to distort them. But by the late twentieth century, the guarding of information and politically incorrect views had become almost impossible. Havel's essays and the writings of other dissidents slipped across the borders to be published widely in the West. How much the Velvet Revolution was the result of Havel's efforts in writing and living in the truth is hard to determine, but the influence of his efforts appears to have been significant. Certainly they launched him into his open public role of the nineties.

In 1985 Havel wrote in an essay for the peace conference in Amsterdam:

A trace of the heroic dreamer, something mad and unrealistic is hidden in the very genesis of the dissenter perspective. In the very nature of things, the dissident is something of a Don Quixote. . . . He writes, cries out, screams, requests, appeals to the law—and all the time he knows that, sooner or later, they will lock him up for it. (*Living,* p. 192)

When he wrote this, he had long been such a dreamer. When he became president, he remained a dreamer, but one who now faced the responsibility for realizing some of those dreams. The circumstances of his political activity were reversed. He had become one of the powerful. But Havel, I think, would rather attribute power to the truth than to himself. Over Prague Castle when he is present flies the banner "Truth Overcomes."[13]

Nonpolitical Politics

What political vision can a dissident have, especially one who lives in a restrictive totalitarian state? One could be an anarchist, a political utopian, a revolutionary who, like Marx or Lenin or Trotsky, sees the coming of a new classless society brought about by violence. Or one could picture a benevolent monarchy that combines the best consequences of hierarchical control with a minimum of infringement on individual human rights. None of these were Havel's dream. Rather, the dissidents in Czechoslovakia with whom Havel had the most affinity were democrats, not first imagining that they would overthrow the current communist regime and return the country to self-government but promoting the development of a parallel culture, a civil society operating as much as possible outside the control of the state authorities. What they were calling for was a nonpolitical politics.[14]

The crucial question for Havel, as he suddenly found himself at the head of an open rebellion and was whisked into Prague Castle as the president of a newly formed republic, was whether this political vision could sustain him not as one of the powerless but as one of the powerful. Now that we can look back from the perspective of the ensuing decade, we can see that Havel has largely maintained his vision. Though he had a major hand in the drafting of the constitution and has paid close attention to proposed changes, especially those involving presidential power, he has refused to join a political party.

The president of the Czech Republic does not have as much power as the American president. His role is somewhere between that of the U.S. president and that of the present British monarch; it is more than ceremonial but less than commanding. Occasionally one hears his self-critical regrets that he did not attempt to take more political control when he first took office. He believes that he let power for the good slip from his hands into those of men like Václav Klaus, the first prime minister, with whom he has differed markedly on economic policy and other matters. Still, it has been hard for Havel to live according to nonpolitical politics as president and, of course, he has not really done so. Every act of a president is political.

Interestingly, other Czech politicians and the Czech people seem to be generally pleased with what Havel has done for them internationally. He has become a symbol of all that is good about their country; his acceptance in the courts and universities of nations around the world has put the Czech Republic on the map. Not that the people are always pleased with the themes of his speeches. Havel's insistence on seeing the Czech Republic (and Slovakia, too, for that matter) as an integral part of an ever more integrated Europe is rejected by Czech and Slovak nationalists. Most have seemed pleased for the Czech Republic to become a member of NATO, but they were much less pleased with Havel's support of the NATO bombing of Serbia in the Kosovo conflict.[15] And it is on these sorts of international themes that Havel's speeches seem more and more to focus. However, his emphasis on responsibility to Being remains implicit throughout these speeches. Responsibility is the central thread binding all of his speeches to his basic worldview.

The Intellectual as Political Dreamer

There is no doubt that Václav Havel is a dreamer—a dreamer in a sense that he not only admits to but glories in. In fact, he dreams on principle (*Art*, p. 34). He is not, however, a dreamer who sees what he wants in the future and then by sheer power and the manipulation of ideology launches a plan—of five years or fifty—to see that it comes to be. That he soundly repudiates. We have seen it tried with National Socialism, Marxist-Leninist communism and Stalinism, and with what went by the name of "real socialism" or "normalization" in recent Czech history. The evidence is in; no one should try it again.

In large measure Havel's dreams for his nation are neither odd nor unrealistic; rather, they are mostly ideals we have taken for granted in the

West.[16] "Perhaps we can all agree," Havel writes, "that we want a state based on rule of law, one that is democratic (that is, with a pluralistic political system), peaceful, and with a prospering market economy" (*Summer*, p. 17). He dreams as well of "a shared feeling of co-responsibility for public affairs"; "a new generation of young, well-educated politicians, whose outlook has not been distorted by the era of totalitarianism"; an independent judiciary; a courteous police force; the privatization of most businesses and services; towns that recover from the nondescript grayness left by totalitarian city planning; and the end of high-rise apartments.

In a simple, dramatic way Havel, in his first official speech to the nation, outlined his vision for the new Czechoslovakia:

> I dream of a republic independent, free, and democratic, of a republic economically prosperous and yet socially just, in short, of a humane republic which serves the individual and which therefore holds the hope that the individual will serve it in turn. Of a republic of well-rounded people, because without such it is impossible to solve any of our problems, human, economic, ecological, social or political. (*Open*, p. 396)

Eight years later Havel expanded on this dream in an eloquent speech devoted entirely to his conception of the type of civil society he would like to see become a reality. In a civil society "citizens participate—in many parallel, mutually complementary ways—in public life, in the administration of public goods and in public decisions." Such a society has "three basic pillars": (1) "free association of people in different types of organizations, ranging from clubs, community groups, civic initiatives, foundations and publicly beneficial organizations up to churches and political parties"; (2) "a strong self-government within the system of public administration" and (3) a system of public and private entities to provide "social welfare, public health, education and the protection of the environment." Such a civil society "generates genuine pluralism and pluralism—leading to competition—produces quality." This pluralism in turn safeguards both tyranny and political chaos. Rather than pretending that government can provide all things to all people, pluralism frees citizens to provide well for themselves. Havel concludes his list with what he calls civil society's most important aspect: "It enables people to realize themselves truly and entirely as the beings that they potentially are, that is, as the species called *zoon politicon,* or political animal." People are not just "manufacturers, profit-makers or consumers." They are creatures who want to live in community, to have and take responsibility. "Humanity constitutes a subject of conscience, of moral order, of love for our fellow humans."[17]

On an international scale, Havel envisions the universal adoption of human rights, nations without nationalism, in fact, a "planetary democracy" that puts people and individuals before states. His vision, as he described it to the National Press Club in Canberra, Australia, in 1995, is vast:

> The only wise course is the most demanding one: we must start systematically transforming our civilization into a truly multicultural civilization, one that will allow all to be themselves while denying none the opportunities it offers, one that strives for the tolerant coexistence of different identities, one that clearly articulates the things that unite us and that could develop into a set of shared values and standards enabling us to lead a creative life together. (*Art*, p. 193)

Four years later Havel restated that vision, setting it in the tragic context of the war in Kosovo. Havel considered NATO's intervention "the first war that has not been waged in the name of 'national interests,' but rather in the name of principles and values"—the value of the individual over the value of the state.[18]

Havel is not committed to democracy as it is now experienced either in the Czech Republic or the West. Today's democratic world has a "limited ability . . to step beyond its own shadow, or, rather, the limits of its own present spiritual and intellectual condition and direction, and thus its limited ability to address humanity in a genuinely universal way" (*Art*, p. 179). But to do better our culture will need to reroot itself in Being. And that might well begin with the politicians.

> It is my impression that sooner or later politics will be faced with the task of finding a new, postmodern face. A politician must become a person again, someone who trusts not only a scientific representation and analysis of the world, but also the world itself. He must believe not only in sociological statistics, but in real people. He must trust not only an objective interpretation

of reality, but also its soul, not only an adopted ideology, but also his own thoughts; not only the summary reports he receives each morning but his own instincts.

Soul, individual spirituality, firsthand personal insight into things, the courage to be oneself and go the way one's conscience points, humility in the face of the mysterious order of Being, confidence in its natural direction, and, above all, trust in one's own subjectivity as the principal link with the subjectivity of the world—these, in my view, are the qualities that politicians of the future should cultivate. (*Art*, pp. 92-93)

Havel seems to have experienced something of the transformation he urges for others. He reflects on his first year as president of Czechoslovakia: "I was simply 'pulled forward by Being.' . . . I became 'an instrument of the time.' . . . There was no choice. History—if I may put it this way—forged ahead and through me, guiding my activities" (*Summer*, pp. xvi-xviii). Is history biography? Is biography repeatable? Havel seems to think so or to dream so.

So perhaps we should ask again: Is Havel dreaming? Is any of his vision more likely of realization than the utopias he so soundly rejects? The answer depends almost solely on two factors: whether his worldview is true, or at least true enough to put our culture back on track, and whether people will grasp its truth, or at least act as if they grasped its truth. We will address these issues in the next chapter.

5

A Critical
Analysis of
Havel's Worldview

Being as such—that there is something, not nothing—has become
something that needs justification, something for which arguments
must be advanced and a grounding found. That is not something
that happens necessarily. . . . Once, however, the self-evidence
of the self-evident has been called into question, philosophy has begun.

ERAZIM KOHÁK, JAN PATOČKA

VÁCLAV HAVEL IS A POLITICIAN who calls other politicians—and people around the world—to return to their roots in Being, to seek an ethical
and spiritual transformation of their souls, and on that foundation to
accept responsibility for their lives, for the dignity and welfare of others
and for the restoration of the environment. Havel is, frankly, an evangelist
for Being.

His fervor leaves us with a task. Is he right? Should we seek those
"existential metaexperiences" in which Being speaks to us? Should we
begin to equate our conscience with the voice of Being? Should we, in
short, get on the bandwagon for Being?

We have already seen in chapter three that Havel claims that he is not
a philosopher and that he does not have a comprehensive worldview.[1]
But in spite of his claims to the contrary, Havel presents his philosophic
musings in depth, makes a case for their truth, and calls others to action
on the basis of them. I will try, then, to couch my analysis of Havel's

views at the level of Havel's own presentation, neither raising subtle philosophical questions of concern only to professional philosophers nor avoiding the tough questions that should concern any of us who are listening to his clarion call to responsibility.[2]

The Truth About Being

If one's answer to the first worldview question—What is fundamental reality?—forms the foundation for the rest of one's understanding of the world and of our place in it, then it is most important that the answer we give be true, or as nearly true as possible. So we may well ask: Does Being, as Havel conceives it, exist? Or: Is Being?

These seem like pointless questions if one takes *being* to mean what Havel takes Being in general to mean: Being is the *isness* of what is. Of course, there is such Being, for if there is anything (which there plainly is), then there is Being. So far so good.

But Being as such—that is, Being that lacks any further characteristics—can form no foundation for anything but the brute *isness* of all that is. Being is. We are because Being is. That's it. Characterless Being cannot help us know who we are as a class ("human") or who any of us is as an individual. It can tell us nothing about why we are here or how we should live. We may indeed seem to be "thrown" out from Being, differentiated from both the absolute horizon and from the immediate horizon of our environment. But such Being helps us understand nothing more than our brute being in time.

Though this spare description of our subjective state of existence-in-the-world can be challenged, it may be acceptable as an expression of a primitive, pretheoretical grasp of our situation as human beings. But Havel does not rest his call to responsibility on such a thin concept of Being. Being has depth of character. It is, as we saw in chapter three, infinite, omniscient, incorruptibly moral and seemingly, though not actually, personal.

If Being is all these things, it does have sufficient character to undergird an explanation of why our universe appears orderly; why as human beings we are capable of knowing reality; why we have an innate and powerful sense of right and wrong; and even why we sense that history is heading in a particular, perhaps even determined direction. The assured characteristics of Being—infinity, omniscience, and incorruptible morality—give us most of what we need.[3] And the seemingly—though not actually—personal character of Being can give us the appearance of explaining why we often think that we are here for a reason and why history will end in the triumph of good.

Knowing the Truth About Being

Why, then, does Havel think Being has these rich characteristics? There are two ways to answer this question. Havel gives one answer. I will add a second. Havel's expressly given reason is this: Being has appeared to him in such powerful "existential metaexperiences" that the reality behind the phenomenon must be objectively there. We have already noted the four experiences that exemplify, but do not exhaust, the data for him. There are the tree shimmering in the breeze outside the prison walls in Heřmanice, the powerful stab of conscience on the tram at night, his empathy with the TV weather announcer, and his feelings of failure and guilt over his request for release from prison. These are, as William James describes them, noetic experiences that are so strong that the reality they point to simply must—as far as the subject is concerned—exist:

> Mystical states seem to those who experience them to be also states of knowledge. They are states of insight into depths of truth unplumbed by the discursive intellect. They are illuminations, revelations, full of significance and importance, all inarticulate though they remain; and as a rule they carry with them a curious sense of authority for after-time.[4]

James is willing to accord some limited credence to the testimony of mystical experiences, but he notes that while they may have "absolute" authority for those who have had them, they have no authority at all for those who do not have them.[5] So if we take a Jamesian approach, we might conclude that Havel's own belief is justified, but that there is no reason we should take his view for our own.

Havel, however, is not a Jamesian pragmatist. So to Havel's first reason for his conclusions about Being we must add a second one—the source of Havel's conception. Havel works within the framework of the continental phenomenology of philosophers like Martin Heidegger and Jan Patočka.

For them Being takes an active part in human knowing: it reveals itself. Being produces the phenomena that point back to itself. As a young man Havel read Patočka's *The Natural World as Philosophical Problem* with "feverish excitement." Then, he says, "I studied thoroughly everything of his I could get my hands on."[6] Later Havel and Patočka became friends. Havel read Heidegger in prison in Heřmanice, if not before.[7] And, as we noted previously, he uses three distinctive terms from Heidegger *Sein* (Being), *Dasein* (existence-in-the-world), and *Geworfenheit* (thrownness), doing so with meanings similar to Heidegger's, or so it seems to me. When Havel's views are compared to Patočka's and Heidegger's, the similarities are immediately evident.

So Havel understands Being as he does because he has learned about it first from Patočka and then, in due course, from Heidegger. When he attempts to explain his especially striking experiences, therefore, he identifies them as "existential metaexperiences" and interprets them as Being breaking in on him. Through them he is being re-rooted in Being.

There is no particular objection to first being exposed to a philosophy or worldview and then understanding one's experience in its terms. This, I take it, happens to every thoughtful human being. We are not the originators of the ideas by which we first find ourselves living, or of those by which we choose to live after a little or even a lot of thought. Children raised in a distinctly Hindu home will be Hindu in basic orientation, or they will be in rebellion against Hinduism, before they are anything else. What is a matter of concern, however, is whether the worldview that one has adopted is true.

So, then, what evidence is there for the truth of Havel's notion of Being? At least three approaches can be taken. The first is to analyze the whole system within which the notion of Being fits. Is it internally consistent? Second, does the notion of Being actually explain what it claims to explain? And third, is there any particular evidence that tends to confirm this notion? In short, is Havel's explanation the best explanation of all the data at hand?

As to the entire system of which the concept of Being is a part—in its fully Heideggerian version, let's say—I am not prepared to comment. Heidegger is notoriously difficult to understand. To quote Roger Scruton:

"It is impossible to summarise Heidegger's work, which no one has claimed to understand completely. In the next chapter [of Scruton's *A Short History of Modern Philosophy*] I shall give reasons for thinking that it may be unintelligible." While Heidegger clearly makes the claim that his system describes the world as such, Scruton explains, he "does not give any arguments for the truth of what he says."[8] For our purposes we can fortunately leave the question of Heidegger's system open. It is enough to note that if his sources give no argument for their own truth, the reasons for Havel's view—if there are any—will have to come from elsewhere.

Actually, Havel does give evidence: the evidence of his mystical or quasimystical experiences. For Havel these experiences are determinative. Should they be?

Let us return to Havel's own reflection on the most mystical of the four experiences he describes—his experience of the shimmering tree (*Living*, p. 331; see pp. 57-58 above for entire text). As he watches the tree, its leaves trembling and shining, he is taken into a "state outside of time." Everything beautiful that he has ever seen seems "co-present" to him; everything seems reconciled and at peace. Even though he is physically still in prison, he feels that he can face the future. Behind all these phenomena he senses and is amazed at the sovereignty of Being; it gives him a "dizzying sensation of tumbling endlessly into the abyss of its mystery." He is even "struck by love," though for whom or what he cannot tell. Havel draws from these phenomena the conclusion that it is Being in which he is immersed, that he is standing "at the 'edge of the finite,' " that he is supremely happy and "in harmony with the world and himself." At this point Being not only is the *isness* of what is, but also *sovereign* and *benign,* the perpetrator of a generic *love without specific object.* There is thus still much mystery to Being.

As a result of the second of these four experiences, his attack of conscience on the tram at night, he is able to see more deeply into the character of Being (*Living,* pp. 345-46; see p. 58 above for the entire text). Here he hears "the voice of Being" itself. He sees Being as omniscient, omnipresent, entirely incorruptible, the highest authority, Law itself. Being not only is eternal but makes Havel eternal as well. Moreover, Being addresses him through his conscience as if Being were personal.

In short, the phenomena of Havel's conscience implies that there is a transcendent that is obligating him to act as he should. He is riding a tram; he therefore owes the transport company for a ride; he should pay what is due. But he should do this because he is responsible to something higher than anything that is merely immanent, that is in his immediate horizon (himself, friends, society). This transcendent Being seems identical to a fully theistic God. All the characteristics are there, including personality.

Should not Havel, then, conclude that the transcendent is such a God? There is nothing in his immediate experience to lead him to think otherwise. It is only as he reflects that he hesitates and then decides not to do so. For many "subtle reasons" he declines to call Being *God*. Among these reasons he lists a vague sense of shame before someone he can't identify. In fact, he wonders if the entire experience of the "personality" of Being is merely a projection of his own subjective self.

So, while Being manifests characteristics that seem to demand a commitment to theism, Havel avoids the theistic conclusion by shifting his attention from Being (as an objective existent to which phenomena point) to himself (as a reflector on his conscious experience). The personal appearance of Being, he concludes, is more likely a projection of his own experience. He is content to say, "the Being of the universe, at moments when we encounter it on this mystical level, suddenly assumes a personal face and turns this, as it were, toward us" (*Living*, p. 346).

Two questions immediately arise. First, how does Havel know which phenomena point outward to an objective reality outside himself and which merely reflect an inward sense without an external cause? Havel gives no suggestions as to how this might be answered, and I can't think of any. It appears that such a distinction has no foundation. Any attempt to decide which phenomena point outward and which remain merely subjective is gratuitous. Worse, the decision is open to manipulation by mere desire rather than motivated by a passion for the truth.

Second, what does it mean to have a sense of *shame* before an impersonal transcendent? Does not the sense of shame itself demand a presence of the personal? Surely one cannot rationally be ashamed in the presence of the completely impersonal.

Let's say that I suddenly find that my trousers are unzipped. I am ashamed because I am concerned about what people might think about me. I experience a great sense of relief when I realize that no one could have seen the result of my lapse. The shame disappears and is replaced by simple disgust at my inattention to modest detail. But when I misbehave and I think that I am observed by a God who is infinite, personal, omniscient and good, I have not only a sense of shame, but also a sense of guilt. When I am alone and measure my actions against my ideals, I can, of course, feel ashamed. But that is because I have a sense of what I ought to do. My shame is here more like guilt. I should do what I have not done. I have done what I should not do. But what accounts for this feeling that is more profoundly disturbing than shame?

In his internal response to his failure to live in the truth when he wrote his request for release from prison, Havel is clear that the Being who "spoke to him" appeared as personal:

> I have my failure to thank for the fact that for the first time in my life I stood—if I may be allowed such a comparison—directly in the study of God himself: never before had I looked into his face or heard his reproachful voice from such proximity, never had I stood before him in such profound embarrassment, so humiliated and confused, never before had I been so deeply ashamed or felt so powerfully how unseemly anything I could say in my own defense would be. (*Letters*, p. 253)

It is always good to be humble when speaking of God. The Hebrews would not even voice his name. So Havel's feeling of shame may indeed come appropriately from that perception. But if Being has really shown itself to be personal, is it not more honoring to *him* (the impersonal *it* seems to be inappropriate) to see this and admit it?

One thing we can easily grant to Havel: We all have a moral sense. We all act as if some things are right and others wrong. The moral sense is universal. What is not universal is that, except at a very basic level, the specific content of that moral sense varies from person to person, tribe to tribe, country to country, and time to time. But this is not relevant. The universality of the moral sense makes one of the more convincing cases for the existence of a personal God. It appears, in fact, that when Havel argues from his own "existential metaexperiences," he is making just such a case for transcendent Being.

The argument can be stated like this: (1) We all act as if we believe that there are absolute standards for right and wrong; (2) these standards are not a part of the natural order (like sticks and stones or even people); (3) we do not create these standards—they exist apart from us as obligations on our behavior (one cannot be obligated to oneself); (4) obligation by its very nature requires a person to whom the obligation is due (one cannot be obligated to an impersonal, abstract rule, such as, "Thou shalt not kill"). [9] Havel accepts the first three of these but not the fourth. For Havel, Being is not personal, yet we are responsible to Being. This, I suggest, cannot be so.

One could rejoin that the law of gravity is a standard outside us, that we did not make it, but we have to live by it. True, but we cannot break the law of gravity. It is a natural fact that on earth unsupported objects fall. If I try to break the law of gravity, say, by jumping off a ten-story building, I do not really break the law. Rather, my fall and my mangled body exemplify it. The moral law, on the other hand, can be broken. We can choose to commit murder. If there is a painful result, it will not be because of the natural order of the universe, but because I "personally" or "psychologically" find myself to be in pain or because some other people or some reigning deity causes me to suffer. It is not so much that I am obligated to the law of gravity as it is that the law of gravity is one of the boundary conditions of life itself. If I am obligated to continue to live, I must take careful account of the law of gravity. But the obligation to live will have come from something outside the natural order. Hence if there is any foundation for my thinking that there is a difference between right and wrong, a personal transcendent must exist. In short, the existence of a personal God (theism) is a better explanation for Havel's intense experience of conscience than is his conception of impersonal Being.

One could construct a parallel argument for the existence of a personal God on the basis of the awe Havel feels before the "sovereignty of Being." Something huge but strictly impersonal does not inspire awe, only, perhaps, fear for one's life, especially if that big thing also appears to be dangerous to life and limb. Beautiful sunsets, for example, inspire awe.

Thus, the simple argument: Beautiful sunsets exist; therefore a personal transcendent exists. This argument is not as strong as the argument from the moral sense, but it bears some consideration. It parallels another interesting argument from aesthetics. In their catalog of twenty arguments for the existence of a personal God, philosophers Peter Kreeft and Ronald K. Tacelli list as number seventeen:

> There is the music of Johann Sebastian Bach.
> Therefore, there must be a God.
> You either see this or you don't.[10]

Many Subtle Reasons

Havel, we saw above, says that "there are many subtle reasons" that he is reluctant to equate Being with a God who is personal. But in the section following this he gives only this one we have considered: his fear of over-objectifying the phenomenon of being addressed by a person. Chalk that up to the fact that his prison letters are limited to four pages. He gives other reasons in other letters. He writes, for example, that "human behavior always carries within it . . . traces of an emotional assumption or inner experience of 'the total integrity of being' " (*Letters*, p. 232). This is "an experience of something supremely spiritual." Then he hesitates:

> Nevertheless, I confess I still can't talk of God in this connection: God, after all is one who rejoices, rages, loves, desires to be worshiped: in short, he behaves too much like a person for me. Yet I'm aware of a paradox here: if God does not occupy the place I am trying to define here, it will all appear to be no more than some abstract shilly-shallying. But what am I to do? (*Letters*, p. 233).

Havel is apparently objecting to a theistic God. We could question his understanding of such a God, but let's accept the terms of his objections as he states them. How might a traditional Christian respond to each?

What does it mean for God to *rejoice*? Does it not mean, among other things, that he takes the good that happens with delightful seriousness? It means something to him. He is pleased.

For God to *rage* means that he takes evil with deadly seriousness. God hates evil. His rage expresses this seriousness in terms we can understand as human beings. Rage need not mean uncontrolled anger and vindictiveness. It may well be the necessary flip side of his allowing human beings a large measure of freedom.

For God to *love* means that God intends the very best for us. In fully Christian terms God's love is expressed by Jesus, the Son of God who knew no sin but became sin for us that "we might become the righteousness of God" (2 Corinthians 5:21).

For God to *desire to be worshiped* indicates that God wants us to recognize who he really is. He is our Creator. We owe our very being to him. He gave us freedom. He rescued us when we failed to live righteous lives. He deserves to be worshiped and rejoices when we do so. It may be that God desires us to worship him more for our benefit than for his own.

Havel's Rejection of Christian Theism

Early in his presidency, Havel had to clarify his religious commitment. Some thought that he had converted to Catholicism. He admits to becoming closer friends with some Catholics and Protestants, but he expressly denies conversion to either expression of Christian faith, saying he has not changed his mind from what he wrote in the prison letters (*Disturbing*, pp. 189-90). There Havel explicitly rejects the Christian version of theism. Because his comments expand on those we have just noted, it will be useful to consider them here.

Havel was raised as a Catholic, but he seems never to have made a personal commitment:

> Ever since childhood, I have felt that I would not be myself—a human being—if I did not live in a permanent and manifold tension with this "horizon" of mine, the source of meaning and hope—and ever since my youth, I've never been certain whether this is an "experience of God" or not. Whatever it is, I'm certainly not a proper Christian and Catholic (as so many of my good friends are) and there are many reasons for this. (*Letters*, p. 101)

Havel goes on to give some of these reasons. First, "I do not worship this god of mine and I don't see why I should. What he is—a horizon without which nothing would have meaning and without which I would not, in fact, exist—he is by virtue of his essence, and not thanks to some strong-arm tactics that command respect" (*Letters*, p. 101).

A Christian theist might respond, "Yes and no." Of course God is what he is by virtue of his essence. This is at least part of what was meant when the voice from the burning bush told Moses, "I AM WHO I AM" (Exodus 3:14). Yes, God is omnipotent; he is power. But *strong-arm tactics* is clearly a loaded term that denigrates God. God is not to be worshiped because he forces it. And his commands to worship are not justified by the power that could enforce them. We are to worship God because he is worthy of worship, worthy by virtue of his love, goodness, creativity and, yes, humility. He does not force us, he woos us; in Jesus he dies for us. "Worthy is the Lamb, who was slain" (Revelation 5:12).

Havel gives a second reason:

> By worshiping him in some model fashion, I don't think I could improve either the world or myself, and it seems quite absurd to me that this "intimate-universal" partner of mine—who is sometimes my conscience, sometimes my hope, sometimes my freedom and sometimes the mystery of the world—might demand to be worshiped or might even judge me according to the degree to which I worship him (*Letters*, p. 101).

But isn't the Christian notion of an infinite-personal God what is needed to make sense of Havel's feeling of an "intimate-universal" partner? The God of the Bible, especially as he is revealed in Jesus, is both universal and intimate. But it is not just his universality that makes him worthy of worship; it is also his character of compassion and mercy. If he did not want Havel to worship him by acknowledging who he really is, he would not be fully good, would he? Why bridle at worship? If an artist can be justly praised for his painting, a dramatist for his plays, why not a creator for his creation and a redeemer for his redemption?

Perhaps Havel's worship of God would improve the world, perhaps not. The issue is of no matter. It is much like Havel's advice to those powerless who speak the truth: perhaps it will help, perhaps not. One thing is sure: if we do not worship, nothing will come of it; but if we do, we will be acknowledging God for who he is, and that is worth doing regardless.

Havel's third reason is a rejection of external authority: "Related to this is my constant compulsion to reconsider things—originally, authentically, from the beginning—that is, in an unmediated dialog with this god of mine; I refuse to simplify matters by referring to some respected, more material authority, even if it were the Holy Writ itself" (*Letters*, p. 101).

The question is, of course, what is Holy Writ, and is it worth considering? Even if Holy Writ were only the words of fallible people, it would be worth considering for its rich mine of ethics and suggestive notions. If it is or even contains God's word to us, then to ignore it is to ignore a major source of knowledge and wisdom. So why not do both—"reconsider things—originally, authentically, from the beginning" and take into account the best that has been thought and said by others? The Scriptures will at least be within that category.

Finally, Havel's fourth reason involves self-analysis:

> When it gets right down to it, I am a child of the age of conceptual, rather than mystical, thought and therefore my god as well—if I am compelled to speak of him (which I do very unwillingly)—must appear as something terribly abstract, vague and unattractive (all the more so since my relationship to him is so difficult to pin down). But it appears so only to someone I try to tell about him—the experience itself is quite vivid, intimate and particular, perhaps (thanks to its constantly astonishing diversity) more lively than for someone whose "normal" God is provided with all the appropriate attributes (which often enough can alienate more often than drawing one closer). (*Letters*, pp. 101-2)

Havel's self-characterization seems a bit disingenuous. Yes, he is highly conceptual—that is, he is a thinker—but he is also open to preconceptual, "existential metaexperience." And when he speaks of the "god" he encounters in these experiences, his language does not reflect "something terribly abstract, vague and unattractive"—quite the contrary.

Havel has drawn a false dichotomy: He does not have to choose between an alienating personal God and an unalienating impersonal God. True, so much that passes for a "normal" God is often alienating. But the God of the Bible, especially God as we see him manifested in Jesus, is hardly alienating in and of himself. People experience alienation only when they realize that they are dealing with a holy God and are under his judgment and not yet under his mercy. Jesus' call is the epitome of mercy: "Come to me, all you who are weary and burdened, and I will give you rest. Take my yoke upon you and learn from me, for I am gentle and humble in heart, and you will find rest for your souls. For my yoke is easy and my burden is light" (Matthew 11:28).

In other words, there is, I think, less to object to in the theistic concept of God than Havel wishes to acknowledge. To affirm a fully theistic God, he would not have to eliminate anything of his experience or understanding of Being. A theistic God would, in fact, be a more consistent understanding of Havel's self-confessed experience.

So is there something more to Havel's reluctance to affirm a fully personal God? We may find a suggestion in Havel's remark that "if God does not occupy the place I am trying to define here, it will all appear to be no more than some abstract shilly-shallying" (Letters, p. 233). He seems to realize that he may be rejecting such a God because he simply doesn't want to deal with a Person who could genuinely hold him responsible for his actions and could back that with unhappy consequences. More than one person has rejected the biblical God, or has hesitated in abstract shilly-shallying, because they have not wanted to contemplate the possibility of eternal damnation. Havel, of course, never suggests this. Is this a lack of candor? He is so honest about so much, that would be hard to prove.

Human Nature

Havel's description of human nature is not easy to untangle. Couched in Heideggerian terms, it seems at times almost as impenetrable as Heidegger himself. Nonetheless, the outlines are clear. Human beings are "thrown" out from Being and find themselves separate from their home in Being. This constitutes the Fall (to use Christian terminology, which both Heidegger and Havel do). Our problem as human beings, then, is an ontological one. We are no longer one with our origin. In our alienation from Being we act as if we were the arbiters of our own destiny, knowing, as we face death, that we can't have the eternality we crave. As we noted above, neither Havel nor Heidegger gives an argument for this. Each just states it, and Havel, at least, sees his "existential metaexperiences" in these terms.

Because Being does not choose, in this view, to reveal itself in human words or in human form, the best case that can be made for Havel's understanding of human nature will be to determine how well it accounts for our common experience as human beings. I suggest that for several reasons it is inadequate.

First, this view of human nature takes a romantic view of the reality of the world that we experience. The evidence within the natural world is that Being is not only benevolent. Russian dissident Joseph Brodsky puts it well in his open letter to Havel: "The metaphysical order, Mr. President, should it really exist, is pretty dark, and its structural idiom is its part's mutual indifference. The notion that man is dangerous runs, therefore, closest to that order's implications for morality. . . . At any rate, it seems more prudent to build society on the premise that man is evil rather than the premise of his goodness."[11]

Human nature—its evil as well as its good—is not so well explained by an ontological alienation from Being as it is by a moral alienation from a righteous God who created human beings in his image and granted them freedom to rebel (which they have). Havel does not, I think, address the problem of evil as such in his writings.[12] If Being is good, why did the beings "thrown" out from it not act as if they were creatures of goodness? Is Being actually the repository of those moral standards by which human lives will be judged? The problem of evil is a major issue in theistic philosophy. It should be so for any view that labels fundamental reality as solely good. Given his experience in prison, it is odd that Havel has not considered this issue.

Second, the fact that Havel's entire explanation of the appearance of humans is speculative should cause any thoughtful person to ask, Why should I accept Havel's explanation of the human condition? What strengths does it have that alternate explanations do not have? Christian theism, for example, sees the essential problem of human nature not as ontological but as moral. Our problem is not that we are not God. Rather, our problem is that we have been given by God the freedom to decide against God and we have done so.[13]

The Goodness of Being

With this critique of Havel's view of human nature, we need to look again at his pretheoretical commitment to the goodness of Being. Brodsky has raised a significant objection: "The metaphysical order is . . . pretty dark." In fact, it is both dark and light. There is, in accord with our moral sense, a lot of good in the world and a lot of evil. Manicheanism simply affirms that and tries to live with it: Good and evil are equal and opposite forces in the universe. Would not, in fact, Manicheanism accord better with some of the details of Havel's system than would his own brand of phenomenal ethics? For example, Havel says on a number of occasions that the soul is immortal: "Human existence . . . will endure, once and for all, in the 'memory of Being' " (Letters, p. 139; cf., p. 155). What does Being remember? Both the good and the evil? Does this "memory" transform Being itself? How does Being deal with this "memory of evil"? Does the memory of the vilest of human beings reside alongside the memory of the best of the best human beings? Shouldn't we expect some reflection on these questions from Havel?

Havel the Politician: Utopian, Dreamer or Visionary?

Since the early days of his presidency, Havel's popularity has waned both with ordinary citizens and within the political arena where power struggles are the order of the day. Marek Mudrik surveys the Czech media's growing disillusionment with Havel, a disillusionment that reflects that of the populace at large. Mudrik notes, for example, that in December 1998 a poll by the Institute for the Research of Public Opinion found that "55% of nearly 1200 respondents said that Havel should think about leaving office (allegedly for health reasons)."[14] Steven Erlanger reports that in the fall of 1999 Havel's approval rating "hovered around 52%." Reflecting on the tenth anniversary of the Velvet Revolution, Erlanger writes, "The idolized heroes of Communism's collapse—sometimes unlikely leaders like Lech Welesa in Poland, Havel and even Boris N. Yeltsin of Russia—have found themselves chewed apart, with their historical reputations more pitted the longer they have remained in office."[15]

On a practical level, two major criticisms of Havel were launched early and continue to be held against him. In the words of Jacques Rupnik, "The first argues that he failed to oppose effectively the breakup of Czechoslovakia. The second claims that he did not voice strongly enough his opposition to Prime Minister Václav Klaus's reduction of the democratic dream of 1989 to the free-market verbiage of the 1990s."[16] These are both judgment calls requiring two premises. First, they require the premise that one republic with two federations is better than two republics, a premise that is not hard to accept. Second, they require the premise that the market economy that has emerged under Klaus has not freed the human spirit as much as a more mixed economy would have done, a premise that is perhaps correct but is considerably harder to maintain, given the nature of the broader European culture. The criticisms also assume that Havel had the political power either to hold the two nations together or to stem the tidal sweep to a full free market.

A third stringent criticism, launched soon after the Velvet Revolution, is that of Elizabeth Kiss who believes that a nonpolitical politics is doomed to fail from the very start. "A primary focus on civil society," she writes, " ignores or devalues the role of traditional political institutions in constructing a stable democratic order."[17] As a dissident Havel's emphasis on the development of a parallel culture played well among dissidents and in the West where the anticommunist us-versus-them dichotomy was applauded. But the emphasis cannot be sustained once *us* has become *them*: "Conceiving the democratic community as civil society worked against the formulation of legislative programs by parties and decisive activity by new governments."[18] I think that Havel now may agree with her. "I let political life run its own course. I think I shouldn't have done that" he said recently, "I should have been more involved."[19] In 1995 one Czech cab driver, commenting on Havel to Edward Ericson, remarked, "Czech people need strong hand." "As he [Havel] embarked on his final term in office, he promised to override his preference for a 'less visible' presidency and to become 'more energetic and more radical.' "[20]

A fourth criticism comes from a man whom Havel has suggested should succeed him as president. Catholic theologian and philosopher Tomás Halík charges that although Havel's "search for truth is a good export for gaining foreign confidence, . . . it has no meaning in people's inner life. It is something nice to hear and occasionally repeat, but it is not taken seriously, it is not felt deeply at all."[21] This could, of course, be said of the thought of almost any outspoken moralist.

What interests me more than these criticisms of Havel's engagement in politics is the intellectual and spiritual foundation he has so often presented as the justification for his political stances. If that foundation is solid, then both the successes and failures of Havel's actions can be set in context. Assessment becomes much easier. If the foundation is not solid, then Havel, in spite of his disclaimer, becomes another in a long line of utopian dreamers. So is he a misty-eyed dreamer? Or is he a prophetic visionary whose proposals for the future are, after all, realistic? Must we only wait for the vision to realize itself?

If we mean by a utopian a person who casts his picture of the future in an ideology which either by being spoken or believed brings about what it pictures or does so by forcing its vision on the world by violence, Havel is not a utopian. His hatred of ideology spans the years of his adult life. If a dreamer is a person whose ideals cannot be realized at all, then Havel is not a dreamer. If, however, a dreamer is a person who has ideals that he would like to see embodied in social reality, Havel is surely that. Much of what he would like to see in the developing Czech Republic is already embodied in democracies elsewhere. Some of what he dreamt of in 1990 is a reality in the new millennium. But not all.

The more problematic question, of course, is whether Havel's dreams are prophetic, whether Being is not only omniscient, omnipresent and good, but also intent on continuing to reveal itself in "existential metaexperiences" that will lead to a transformation of human nature. This, I think, is highly dubious. For Being to reasonably inspire the hope that it inspires in Havel and to inspire the confidence with which Havel speaks to the rest of us about the future, it must be more personal than Havel believes it to be. Havel quotes Heidegger: "Only a God can save us now" (*Living*, p. 114).[22] Whatever Heidegger meant by this, only a personal God would be able to do what is necessary. When Havel bases his hope on impersonal Being, therefore, he remains a dreamer of unrealistic, unrealizable dreams.[23] In short, the fundamental flaw in Havel as a politician is not political, but metaphysical.

There is much in Havel's political vision with which to agree. He wants what so many of us want, and he has an amazing ability to encourage us toward the realization of goals to which we all can wholeheartedly subscribe. Moreover, despite the passion with which he pursues a role as a morally responsible intellectual politician, he is a humble man. It may indeed be his humility that is his ultimate saving grace. This we will examine in the final chapter.

6_____

The Intellectual
as Franz Kafka's
Doppelgänger?

It was wonderful when nobody was interested in me—
when nobody expected anything from me, nobody urging me to do
anything—I just browsed around the second-hand bookshops—
studying the modern philosophers at my leisure—spending
the nights making notes from their works—taking walks in the park
and meditating—why can't I change my name to Nicholas, say,
and forget everything and start a completely new life?

LEOPOLD NETTLES IN *LARGO DESOLATO*

V ÁCLAV HAVEL, THE MAN: WHAT AN ENIGMA! Of course, that could be
said about anyone, famous or not. What do we know of another? What
do we really understand? What do we know about ourselves? Not much.

But we do try to know others and to know ourselves. In fact, we spend
more time pondering ourselves than is healthy for us. Of course each of
us is closer to our own self than to anyone other than an omniscient (or at
least rather intelligent) God. But are we good observers? Do we judge
well? Having raised the question of our own self-knowledge, do we not
begin to doubt our own self-assessment? I doubt mine.

In fact, I doubt anyone's self-assessment. I doubt it, but I am fascinated by it as well. "Who do you think you are?" we shout at those who
impose on us. "Tell me about yourself," we often say to new or potential
friends. We listen, we evaluate, and we wait to see our judgment con-

firmed by deepening our relationship.

So, Václav Havel, we ask, "Who do you think you are?" Havel is not long in replying. He has made many statements of self-assessment, most of which, whether accurate or not, compose a consistent picture. We will look briefly at that sketch and comment tentatively on its accuracy.

President Kafka

For me Havel's most astonishing piece of writing is the acceptance speech he delivered upon receiving an honorary doctorate from Hebrew University in April 1990, soon after becoming his nation's president. His speech opens with a traditional statement of thankfulness and surprise at being awarded such a prestigious honor. But tradition quickly abates and the speech turns into something very unusual indeed:

> Because of my rather sporadic education, I suffer from feelings of unworthiness, and so I accept this degree as a strange gift, a continuing source of bewilderment. I can easily imagine a familiar-looking gentleman appearing at any moment, snatching the newly acquired diploma from my hands, taking me by the scruff of my neck, and throwing me out of the hall, because it has all been a mistake, compounded by my own audacity. (*Art*, p. 29)

And his audacity immediately becomes evident, for Václav Havel, a Gentile speaking to a Jewish audience, quickly associates himself with Franz Kafka, a Jew: "I want to take this opportunity to confess my long and intimate affinity with one of the great sons of the Jewish people, the Prague writer Franz Kafka." Admitting that he has not read all of Kafka's works and is not much interested in books about him, he makes the connection to Kafka even more intimate: "I sometimes feel that I'm the only one who really understands Kafka, and that no one else has any business trying to make his work more accessible to me." He even claims that he needn't read Kafka himself because "I already know what's there. I'm even secretly persuaded that, if Kafka did not exist, and if I were a better writer than I am, I would have written the works myself."[1]

These are audacious remarks, aren't they? Can he be serious or is he just using ironic hyperbole that will be revealed later when he says, in effect, "Just kidding." What follows, however, shows that Havel is serious. In Kafka, Havel says, "I have found a large portion of my own experience of the world, of myself, and of my way of being in the world." He lists several specific aspects of this experience.

> One of them [forms of experience] is a profound, banal and therefore utterly vague sensation of culpability, as though my very existence were a kind of sin. Then there is a powerful feeling of general alienation, both of my own and one that relates to everything around me that helps to create such feelings; an experience of unbearable oppressiveness, a need constantly to explain myself to someone, to defend myself, a longing for an unattainable order of things, a longing that increases as the terrain I walk through becomes more muddled and confusing. I sometimes feel the need to confirm my identity by sounding off at others and demanding my rights. Such outbursts are, of course, quite unnecessary, and any response fails to reach the right ears and vanishes into the black hole that surrounds me. Everything I encounter displays to me its absurd aspect first. I feel as though I am constantly lagging behind powerful, self-confident men whom I can never overtake, let alone emulate. I find myself essentially hateful, deserving only of mockery. (*Art*, p. 30)

This is an astounding confession. Havel's association with Kafka is with Kafka's fantastic, inexplicable world, not with the artistic craft of the writer, but with the world of his creation, a world Havel experiences—as perhaps did Kafka—as utterly absurd. Readers of Kafka recall, as they hear this, the odd, incoherent world of *The Castle* and *The Trial*, the physically painful world of "In the Penal Colony" with its torture machine that writes vague charges of guilt on the naked body, stripping it to the bone. They see vivid images of Gregor Samsa in "The Metamorphosis," changed from a traveling salesman into a cockroach for no apparent reason. As in the parable of "The Watchman," Havel confesses not to feeling guilty for something specific, but to feeling guilty of guilt itself.[2]

Havel's confession in Jerusalem was not his first. From his early plays to his latest speeches as an international intellectual politician, he has admitted his feelings of inferiority and culpability. He has, as we have already seen, taken on the "responsibility for everything" (*Letters*, p. 324). Anyone whose conscience bears that burden is bound to feel guilty, for who can know what the "everything" is that one is responsible for?

Sometimes Havel hints at specifics. He recalls his last conversation with philosopher Jan Patočka, which took place in 1977: "I could not rid myself of a certain shyness in his presence. . . . [In the presence of famous people] I always tended to be rather cramped, somehow continually ashamed, I don't know of what exactly, perhaps of everything: that I am not as educated or as exact in my thinking, or that I have accomplished little so far, that I enjoy unearned attention."[3] Havel's lack of self-confidence pervades his *Letters to Olga* as he contemplates his tendency to bow to authority, to embarrass easily, to feel inadequate among others.[4] We have already noted his specific and intense feelings of guilt for trying to please the authorities without belying his own principles when he petitioned for his release from prison. The effects of this experience are present in *Largo Desolato* and *Temptation,* and I suspect that they were not far below the surface as he spoke in Jerusalem. In 1995 he was still fraught with inner insecurities: "Nobody can possibly have as many doubts about myself as I do" (*Art,* p. 198).

Havel's self-assessment has as much continuity as his worldview. He has not changed his mind; he has not changed his temperament. Still, we think, do we not, How can Havel be as he claims? Has he not shown great courage throughout his life? Has he not stood up to the evil regime? He could easily have become an expatriate in the United States or Europe. He was even offered the chance and refused.[5] Has he not moved from the ranks of the powerless to the height of political power in his country? Did he not say, a few months after his speech in Jerusalem, that he felt that he had become "an instrument of the time" (*Summer,* p. xvii)? For decades has he not been an active evangelist for Being, a loud voice of conscience for local and international politics?

Havel anticipated this response in what he said next to his Israeli audience: "Yes, I admit that superficially I may appear to be the precise opposite of all those Ks—Josef K., the surveyor K., and Franz K.—although I stand behind everything I've said about myself" (*Art,* p. 30).[6] Then he adds:

> I would only add that, in my opinion, the hidden motor driving all my dogged efforts is precisely this innermost feeling of being excluded, of belonging nowhere, a state of disinheritance, of fundamental nonbelonging. Moreover, I would say that it's precisely my desperate longing for order that keeps plunging me into the most improbable ventures. I would even venture

to say that everything worthwhile I've ever accomplished has been done to conceal my almost metaphysical feeling of guilt. The real reason I am always creating something, organizing something, it would seem, is to defend my permanently questionable right to exist. (*Art*, p. 30-31)

With these words we are back again in the deep waters of Havel's negative self-assessment. How can such a person lead a country? we ask. And so does Havel: "If I am a better president than many others would be in my place, it is precisely because somewhere in the deepest substratum of my work lies this constant doubt about myself and my right to hold office" (*Art*, p. 31). Let us not miss the unusual claim. A politician—one of the "ins"—believes he is a better president for thinking that he could not possibly be a president at all. And let us not miss as well the correctness of the observation. The arrogance of power is the inheritance of everyone in power. This time the inheritance is refused. The outwardly powerful is confessing his inner powerlessness. Perhaps this is the only way a good person can hold power. But we have so few examples of this that we cannot make much of an empirical argument for it.

We would have a hard time imagining any of our recent U.S. presidents, except perhaps Jimmy Carter, saying what Havel says:

I am the kind of person who would not be surprised if, in the very middle of my presidency, I were summoned and led off to stand trial before some shadowy tribunal, or taken straight to a quarry to break rocks. Nor would I be surprised if I were suddenly to hear the reveille and wake up in my prison cell, and then, with great bemusement, proceed to tell my fellow prisoners everything that I had dreamed had happened to me in the past six months. (*Art*, p. 31)

Jimmy Carter would, of course, wake up on his peanut farm and have a good laugh with Rosalynn. Havel, however, has not awakened. He has continued as president even though he imagines that his advisers will reprimand him for speaking so frankly. He concludes his speech with words that I think must have been said with a bit of tongue in a bit of cheek: "Once more, I thank you for the honor, and after what I've said here, I'm ashamed to repeat that I accept it with a sense of shame" (*Art*, p. 31).

Kafka's Doppelgänger

Is Havel Kafka's Doppelgänger—his latter-day double? I can think of a dozen reasons why he is not. I will mention only a few. Havel is utterly unlike any of the Ks that he mentioned in his Jerusalem speech. Franz and the surveyor K., for example, were unable to have normal intimate relations with women as much as they desired to. They never married. Václav was successfully married to Olga for years, and when she died, he quickly married Dagmar. Kafka was a quiet loner; Havel is a haunter of pubs, a conversationalist, a performer. Kafka was Jewish and an outsider to much of Czech society; Havel was born a son of privilege and was only later forced to the outside. The surveyor K. was never able to enter the castle; Havel is its chief officer, its philosopher-king, even though he is unusually modest as philosopher and admittedly not very powerful as king.

Perhaps the most radical difference of all, however, stems from a fundamental difference between Kafka's and Havel's approach to the world of public affairs. Ivan Klíma sketches the turbulent times in which Kafka lived: "When he was thirty-one, a world war broke out, and though he did not have to enlist, he could not escape its consequences. The level of hunger and misery in Prague was difficult to imagine. Mutilation, pain and violent death were all around him." After this came the first democratic government of Czechoslovakia, more nearby "revolutions in Hungary and Germany, . . . and civil war in Russia." Other writers reacted directly to these events. But not Kafka: "On 2 August 1914, there are only two sentences in his diary: 'Germany has declared war on Russia.— Swimming in the afternoon.' "[7]

How unlike Havel is this combination of notions! They seem utterly incommensurate. But then, as Klíma points out, "Kafka was not at all an intellectual author." He didn't try to be. It is not that Kafka did not think. Rather, he thought like a storyteller—in terms of dramatic narrative and vivid images; the story and images are often all there are in his works.[8] They summon up in the reader all sorts of profound intellectual questions, but the questions are not answered. The story, the images, the intense sense that something important is going on: these are all.

In Havel's works, even in the absurdist plays that are most Kafkaesque

(*The Garden Party* and *The Memorandum*), there lurks offstage the hint that the world of the play is not the only world, that behind it all Being is there with its intentions and its morality.

Even more significant differences separate Kafka's and Havel's sense of the universe. This is, after all, what has attracted Havel to his great Prague predecessor. Kafka's literary worlds, the secondary worlds he creates, are unremittingly dense, dark, impenetrable, intriguing but unyielding to rational analysis. Josef K. in *The Trial* cannot learn what he is charged with. His only assurance is that he is guilty. Havel senses the same thing, and displays the same sense of absurdity in his plays. But these plays are the bottom of the well from which one can see the stars in the daylight. For Kafka there is no well deep enough for the stars to appear.

Havel does more than sense the presence of Being, Being speaks in his conscience on the tram at night. Being lays its glory before him in the shimmering tree. Being unites him to the weather forecaster who has lost audio contact with her audience. Being calls him to live in truth, truth that rests deeply in the subconscious of peasants and others who, rooted in the land, are attuned naturally to Being's presence.

For Kafka God, if there is a God, remains distant. Max Brod, whose biographical reflections on Kafka Havel read with great appreciation in prison, says, "The Absolute is there [for Kafka]—but it is incommensurable with the life of man—this would seem to be a fundamental experience of Kafka's."[9] For Havel, the absurd is not the most fundamental aspect of Being; it is what one must experience before that fundamental aspect can be grasped.

But the issue is not settled by these contrasts. Every outside has an inside, and on the inside Havel may well be Kafka's double. He thinks that he is, and on the inside he is the authority. What is odd is that he tries to take his inside outside. It is that which we doubt. Does he know himself or is he deluded?

Another way to view the evidence Havel provides is to see Havel as Kafka/Havel. The Kafka side is full of self-doubt and guilt. The Havel side penetrates beyond the self-doubt and guilt feelings; it sees the glory of Being and senses its clear ethical voice.[10]

To get a clear view of Havel the man would take a whole book, a book

I will not write. Here it will be enough simply to have raised the question of Havel's self-identity and to have looked at some of the data. To us Havel may remain an enigma. Who Havel is may be high on Havel's list of important questions to answer; it need not be high on anyone else's list. For us the most important issues with regard to Havel are what he thinks reality is, how he thinks we should respond to that reality, and whether he is right.

Introduction, Appreciation, Critique
From the beginning I have thought of this book as an introduction to and an appreciation and critique of primarily the written work of Václav Havel. And I have attempted to do each of these tasks in turn. *Havel* is not a household word in the English-speaking world, but people who do know of or about him have been intrigued that I should have spent so much time reading, thinking and writing about a man whose language is almost as foreign to me now as it was fifteen years ago. But Havel is a man worth knowing. Perhaps he is, in the words of one critic, "arguably the greatest man—artist, anti-Communist dissident, philosopher-states-man—of the last half century."[11] I would love not just to meet Havel but to join him at his favorite café or pub for coffee or the stellar beer for which Czechoslovakia is justly famous. To bandy about with him his concept of Being; to listen to his rejoinders; to often—I should imagine—be challenged, if not bested, with his response; to participate in the life of his imagination; to sit in the audience of *Audience*; to roar with laughter along with his friends; to sense the tension of his life as a dissident playwright, president and intellectual conscience of international politics: these I will never experience, never know on the nerve endings of my life.

But Havel can be known in his works, and that has been my first goal. In Havel's words I have tried to live in the truth about Havel, that is, to know the truth and to tell what I have come to know. If I have done that, I have done most of what is needed to write an appreciation as well as an introduction.

It will also have gone a long way toward being a critique. For Havel, like all of us, is a flawed human being. As noble as is his call to moral responsibility, he has not always been a model of nobility. He has been a chain smoker since his youth, and his body, now scarred from surgery performed to save his life from tobacco, testifies to a lack of wisdom. He did not always live in the truth in his marriage to Olga. These lapses in personal character, however, have not been my concern in this book, and they will not be so now. Nor have I been concerned with any of the details of his politics or even with his political philosophy.

What has been of central concern in this book is Havel's take on life, his worldview. And what has interested me most in his worldview is his concept of *Being,* his word for the transcendent that most who hold such a view are content to call God. Does the transcendent exist as Havel has conceived it? Is this concept coherent? Does Havel's Being possess the characteristics that are necessary to undergird his call to responsibility? Is such Being able to account for the existence of human beings? Are we both rooted in Being and thrown from Being as Havel says? What is Havel's case for the existence of Being? Is it convincing?

My answers to these questions are, of course, found in chapters three and five. I am dubious. I think Havel is mistaken, and at a profoundly significant level. To adequately account for the world as we experience it, I am convinced that a God must exist who is not only infinite, omniscient, omnipresent and exhaustively good, but also omnipotent and personal. Only a God who is personal can hold us morally responsible. Why be good? Because there is an abstract moral principle—like the law of gravity—at the heart of reality? No. Such a law is not binding on a person who has the ability to obey or disobey. Only if the law is backed by a Person can we be obligated. Responsibility requires some *one,* not some *principle* toward which that responsibility lies.

A second line of criticism takes a more personal turn. Throughout his life Havel has been a man of many self-doubts. He has suffered from both an uncertain consciousness and a guilty conscience, the latter being illustrated most in his reflection on the overly clever confession he signed to gain release from prison. Both self-doubt and guilt (the reality of it as well as the feelings) are inadequately addressed by Havel's Being. Most people will confess to some self-doubt and guilt feelings. So the existence of these experiences is not at issue. What is at issue is whether one can really *be* guilty before a principle and, more importantly for one's psychological health, whether one can ever feel forgiven, let alone *be* forgiven, by an impersonal Being. Given the frequency with which Havel reflects on his sense of guilt, it seems that he has not yet put his soul at rest. Would it not be a more adequate response to take Jesus at his word, "Come to me, all you who are weary and burdened, and I will give you rest. Take my yoke upon you and learn from me, for I am gentle and humble in heart, and you will find rest for your souls. For my yoke is easy and my burden is light" (Matthew 11:28-30)?

Havel does not, of course, reject such a God without giving some attention to the issue. And he seems to recognize the power of the notion of a personal God as he quotes Heidegger's startling (for philosophy) words, "Only a God can save us now" (*Living*, p. 114). But neither Havel nor Heidegger has grasped that if these words are to have more than an emotional impact, they require God to be, as Francis Schaeffer so aptly put it, The God Who Is There in a fully personal way. God cannot be just a principle, no matter how noble that principle is. Is it possible that there is such a God? That is both the first and final question.

Notes

Preface
[1]James W. Sire, "An Open Letter to Václav Havel," *Crux,* June 1991, pp. 9-14.
[2]James W. Sire, "Absolutni horizont," *Život víry* (1992), pp. 212-16. Some nine years later I learned that Havel never reads articles or books about himself (Steven Erlanger, "One Europe, 10 Years: Gloom in the Castle," *The New York Times,* November 4, 1999).
[3]Edá Kriseová, *Václav Havel: The Authorized Biography* 4(New York: St. Martin's Press, 1993), p. xv.
[4]Ibid., p. xvi.

Chapter 1: The Unexpected Intellectual
[1]Stanislaw Baranczak, "All the President's Plays," in *Critical Essays on Václav Havel,* ed. Marketa Goetz-Stankiewicz and Phyllis Carey (New York: G. K. Hall & Co., 1999), p. 46.
[2]Steven Erlanger, "One Europe, 10 Years: Gloom in the Castle," *The New York Times,* November 4, 1999.
[3]For information on Havel's life I have relied primarily on Jan Vladislav, "A Short Bio-bibliography of Václav Havel," in *Living;* John Keane, *Václav Havel: A Political Tragedy in Six Acts* (London: Bloomsbury, 1999); and Havel's own casual comments in *Disturbing.*
[4]Keane, *Václav Havel,* p. 101.
[5]Ibid., p. 89. J. L. Fischer was a family friend who had studied at Charles University under T. G. Masaryk; Jiří Paukert lived in Brno and counseled Havel by mail. Both Masaryk and Paukert had become familiar with Havel's untutored interest in philosophy. Paukert says that young Havel was "endowed with 'a thirst for philosophy,' a tendency to synthesize (rather than to analyze), and a good sense of seeing and judging things disinterestedly"; he notes as well Havel's "intellectual agility, quick and sharp thinking, his spiritual clear-sightedness," and his "great charm" (ibid., p. 89).
[6]For a profile of Olga Havel, see Ivana Edwards, "Who is Olga Havel?" *World Monitor,* November 1990, pp. 20-24.
[7]Havel's account of his house arrest and surveillance by ubiquitous and often bumbling police from August 5, 1978, to March 23, 1979, make alternatingly infuriating and humorous reading (see Václav Havel, "Reports on My House Arrest," in *Open,* p. 16).
[8]Vladislav, "Short Bio-bibliography," pp. 304-12.
[9]Theodore Draper, "The End of Czechoslovakia," *The New York Review of Books,* Jan-

uary 28, 1993, p. 26.

[10]See Jacques Rupnik, "Václav Havel," *Civilization*, April/May 1998, pp. 45-49, for a brief summary of Havel's political career.

[11]*Chicago Tribune*, January 21, 1998, and January 27, 1998.

[12]Seen from a different angle, Havel in the 1960s appeared to be a simple hippie, a dropout wearing "ten dollars' worth of clothes and badly needing a haircut" (Keane, *Václav Havel*, p. 7). Keane says that Havel at that time did indeed view himself as "a blue-jeaned poet and essay writer" (Ibid., p. 6).

[13]Havel's appreciation for the Western rock music of the sixties and seventies played a part in his life as a dissident, as he and others organized to protest the censorship of the Plastic People of the Universe. Paul Berman discusses the political dimension of rock music in Czechoslovakia in *A Tale of Two Utopias: The Political Journey of the Generation of 1968* (New York: W. W. Norton, 1996), pp. 219-53.

[14]Stephen Schiff, "Havel's Choice," *Critical Essays on Václav Havel*, ed. Marketa Goetz-Stankiewicz and Phyllis Carey (New York: G. K. Hall & Co., 1999), p. 84.

[15]Ibid., p. 78.

[16]Erlanger, "One Europe."

Chapter 2: The Dramatist as Intellectual

[1]Quoted by Antoine Spire in "Un Entretien avec Václav Havel: Ma prison, mon pays . . ." *Le Monde*, April 10-11, 1983, p. 8, as quoted by Marketa Goetz-Stankiewicz in "Ethics at the Crossroads: The Czech 'Dissident Writer' as Dramatic Character," *Modern Drama*, March 1984, p. 119.

[2]Goetz-Stankiewicz, "Ethics at the Crossroads," p. 119; she is quoting Irving Wardle, "Audience/Private View," *The Times*, February 21, 1977, p. 9; and Siegfried Barth, "Landebühne: Zwei Balbe Lehrstücke," *Neue Hannoversche Zeitung*, April 4, 1977, p. 3.

[3]Another way to put this in the words of Peter Steiner: "By creating a fictional universe, play splits reality from its representation and opens the possibility of transcending the immediate givens of a situation, for reflecting about the world in a detached fashion" (Peter Steiner, "Spectacular Pretending: Havel's *The Beggar's Opera*," in *Critical Essays on Václav Havel*, ed. Marketa Goetz-Stankiewicz and Phyllis Carey [New York: G. K. Hall & Co., 1999], p. 198).

[4]Ian McEwan, "An Interview with Milan Kundera," trans. Ian Patterson, *Granta* 11 (1984): 34.

[5]Marketa Goetz-Stankiewicz discusses what makes a play political in "Variations of Temptation—Václav Havel's Politics of Language," in *Critical Essays on Václav Havel*, ed. Marketa Goetz-Stankiewicz and Phyllis Carey (New York: G. K. Hall & Co., 1999), pp. 228-40; in the same volume, Peter Steiner explains how Havel's version of *The Beggar's Opera* (first conceived by John Gay in eighteenth-century England and then adapted by Bertolt Brecht in the 1920s), though it "was not modernized and deliberately refrained from any direct reference to Czechoslovak reality, still prompted an anti-state political interpretation by the secret police and an arrest of the performers" ("Spectacular Pretending," pp. 184-99). Steiner says Havel's version is "a playful representation of schizophrenia addressed to an audience for which this state of affairs was an everyday reality" (ibid., p. 199).

[6]Phyllis Carey, "Living in Lies: Václav Havel's Drama," *Cross Currents*, Summer 1992, p. 201.

[7]In what follows I do not analyze *The Beggar's Opera* (1975); an English translation was published only as this book went to press (*The Beggar's Opera*, trans. Paul Wilson [Ithaca: Cornell University Press, 2001]). Extensive summaries and critiques of *The Beggar's Opera* can be found in Peter Steiner's "Spectacular Pretending"; Marketa Goetz-Stankiewicz's *The Silenced Theatre: Czech Playwrights Without a Stage* (Toronto: University of Toronto Press, 1979), pp. 63-67; and John Keane's *Václav Havel: A Political Tragedy in Six Acts* (London: Bloomsbury, 1999), pp. 234-40.

[8]Paul I. Trensky says that "In *The Garden Party* the distortion of proverbs is symbolic of the downfall of traditional values. . . . The statements have all the formal features of proverbs—but in other respects the combination of words is purely mechanical. . . . In the world of the Pludeks every turn of speech is possible, since their language is governed not by thought, but only by grammar" ("Havel's *The Garden Party* Revisited," in *Critical Essays on Václav Havel*, ed. Marketa Goetz-Stankiewicz and Phyllis Carey [New York: G. K. Hall & Co., 1999], p. 163).

[9]In a speech delivered to the Union of Czechoslovak Writers conference on June 9, 1965, Havel said, "We live in a time when reality is in conflict with platitude, when a fact is in conflict with an *a priori* interpretation of it" (*Open*, p. 16).

[10]Goetz-Stankiewicz, *Silenced Theatre*, p. 51.

[11]Paul I. Trensky sees in the speech "a parody of Marxian dialectics, referring to the thesis of permanent change" ("Havel's *The Garden Party* Revisited," p. 170). Marketa Goetz-Stankiewicz suggests a more universal meaning: Hugo's speech "is primarily an example of statements nullifying themselves, of circular logic run wild. . . . This is Havel's main concern: the power of language as a perpetuator of systems, a tool to influence man's mind and therefore one of the strongest (though secret) weapons of any system that wants to mould him to become a well-functioning part of a system rather than a free spirit—unpredictable, erring, imaginative, mysterious in his tireless search for truth" (*Silenced Theatre*, p. 53).

[12]Polish dissident and expatriate Czeslaw Milosz describes the Marxist goal as the dream "of changing the state into one huge office" (Czeslaw Milosz, *Native Realm: A Search for Self-Definition*, trans. Catherine S. Leach [Garden City: Doubleday, 1968], p. 188).

[13]Goetz-Stankiewicz, *Silenced Theatre*, p. 52.

[14]Ibid.

[15]Czeslaw Milosz, *Native Realm*, p. 187.

[16]Havel unmasked the deceptive ideological language of post-totalitarian Czechoslovakia in a speech delivered to the Union of Czechoslovak Writers conference on June 9, 1965. "The essence of it [conventionalized, pseudo-ideological thinking] is that certain dialectical patterns are deformed and fetishized and thus become an immobile system of intellectual and phraseological schemata which, when applied to different kinds of reality, seem at first to have achieved, admirably, a heightened ideological view of that reality, whereas in fact they have, without noticing it, separated thought from its immediate contact with reality and thus crippled its capacity to intervene in that reality effectively. . . . From being a means of signifying reality, and of enabling us to come to an understanding of it, language seems to have become an end in itself . . . the duty to name things having been superseded by the duty to qualify things

ideologically. . . . The word—as such—has ceased to be a sign for a category, and has gained a kind of occult power to transform one reality into another" (*Open*, pp. 11-12).

[17]M. C. Bradbrook, "Václav Havel's Second Wind," *Modern Drama*, March 1984, p. 131.

[18]Gerard Manley Hopkins, "God's Grandeur," in *The Poems of Gerard Manley Hopkins*, ed., W. H. Gardner and N. H. Mackenzie, 4th ed. (London: Oxford University Press, 1967), p. 66.

[19]One early literary critic wrote that one of Havel's plays is "a type of absurd ritual in which the act of being and non-being is commemorated" (quoted by Marketa Goetz-Stankiewicz in *The Silenced Theatre*, p. 39).

[20]As Michael L. Quinn points out, Puzuk is Václav Havel's brother Ivan's nickname ("Delirious Subjectivity: Four Scenes from Havel," in *Critical Essays on Václav Havel*, ed. Marketa Goetz-Stankiewicz and Phyllis Carey [New York: G. K. Hall & Co., 1999], p. 217). My guess is that it was chosen here as an in-joke for his family; perhaps getting its relevance from Ivan's work in science and the philosophy of science.

[21]Edá Kriseová, *Václav Havel: The Authorized Biography*, trans. Caleb Crain (New York: St. Martin's Press, 1993), p. 78.

[22]Havel discovered while he was in prison that the authorities were afraid of him (Václav Havel, "It Always Makes Sense to Tell the Truth: An Interview with Jiří Lederer," *Open*, p. 91).

[23] *Protest* is actually a play written in response to Havel's friend Pavel Kohout's Vaněk play *Permit*. See Marketa Goetz-Stankiewicz, ed., *The Vaněk Plays: Four Authors, One Character* (Vancouver: University of British Columbia Press, 1987).

[24]Ivan Klíma, a novelist and a friend of Havel, told novelist Graham Swift in December 1989 "that he did not sign Charter 77, but as many of his friends were signatories and he moved in Charter circles, he was none the less subject to scrutiny. He also implied that not signing Charter 77 might have been a tactical advantage: you could be active without advertising the fact. He was not snubbed [by his fellow writers] for not signing. His position was that as an author he wished to sign only his own texts" (Graham Swift, "Looking for Jiří Wolf," *Granta* 30 [Winter 1990]: p.26).

[25]Stanislaw Baranczak, "All the President's Plays," in *Critical Essays on Václav Havel*, ed. Marketa Goetz-Stankiewicz and Phyllis Carey (New York: G. K. Hall, 1999), p. 55.

[26]Czeslaw Milosz, *Native Realm*, p. 244.

[27]In what follows these words, Havel goes on to deeply self-reflect about the failure of the "'I' of my 'I' " and its attempt to shift responsibility to the "non-I" (*Letters*, p. 349-50). Note too the abundance of terminology reminiscent of Heidegger and other existentialists.

Chapter 3: The Intellect of the Intellectual

[1]Czech journalist Luboš Beniak is quoted as saying that Havel is alone in not shifting his philosophy to suit the political times. In fact, he says, Havel "is the only man who has not changed his philosophy during his whole life" (quoted by Stephen Schiff in "Havel's Choice," in *Critical Essays on Václav Havel*, ed. Marketa Goetz-Stankiewicz and Phyllis Carey [New York: G. K. Hall & Co., 1999], p. 79).

[2]Even during his second term as president, Havel says, "I have not been compelled to

recant anything of what I wrote earlier, or to change my mind about anything" (*Summer*, p. 10). Havel is presumably limiting the scope of his claim to what he thought and said just before he became president, but it applies to another ten or fifteen years before that.

[3]I have developed this concept more fully in my book *The Universe Next Door*, 3rd ed. (Downers Grove, Ill.: InterVarsity Press, 1997), especially chapter one. For a survey of the ways in which the concept of *worldview* has been understood, see James H. Olthuis, "On World Views," in *Stained Glass: Worldviews and Social Science*, ed. Paul A. Marshall, Sander Griffoen and Richard J. Mouw (Lanham, Md.: University Press of America, 1989), pp. 26-40.

[4]Havel likewise refuses to think of himself as a philosopher (*Letters*, pp. 147-48) or original thinker (pp. 375-76), but even a casual scanning of *Letters* will reveal distinctly philosophic terminology and concepts. Havel may have in mind a more European understanding of *Weltanschauung*, perhaps like that of Freud: "an intellectual construction which solves all the problems of existence on the basis of one overriding hypothesis which, accordingly, leaves no questions unanswered and in which everything that interests us finds a fixed place" (Sigmund Freud, "The Question of a Weltanschauung," in *New Introductory Lectures, Standard Edition*, vol. 22 [London: Hogarth Press, 1964], p. 158, quoted by Jean Bethke Elshtain in "A Performer of Political Thought: Václav Havel on Freedom and Responsibility," in *Critical Essays on Václav Havel*, ed. Marketa Goetz-Stankiewicz and Phyllis Carey [New York: G. K. Hall & Co., 1999], p. 114).

[5]Carl Sagan, *Cosmos* (New York: Random House, 1980), p. 4. Sagan goes on to say, "Our feeblest contemplations of the cosmos stir us—there is a tingling in the spine, a catch in the voice, a faint sensation, as if a distant memory, of falling from a height. We know we are approaching the greatest of mysteries." For Sagan the cosmos assumes the position of God, creating the same kind of awe in Sagan, who tries to trigger that awe in his readers and television audience. So-called science thus becomes religion, some say the religion of scientism. See Jeffrey Marsh, "The Universe and Dr. Sagan," *Commentary*, May 1981, pp. 64-68.

[6]See, for example, Havel's *Living*, pp. 62, 67, 69, 154-55, 158; "Faith in the World," *Civilization*, April/May 1998, p. 52; and *Disturbing*, p. 54. Such terms continue to appear in his speeches as president: see, for example, *Art*, pp. 18, 79-80, 100, 106,164, 170-72, 175, 196, 220, 241-42, 250. See also the following speeches, which are available at the Prague Castle website: "Address by Václav Havel, President of the Czech Republic, to the French Senate" (March 3, 1999) <www.hrad.cz/president/Havel/speeches/1999/0303_uk>; Speech at the Vatican (September 18, 1999) <www.hrad.cz/president/speeches/index_uk>.

[7]In *Letters*, pp. 122-24, Havel speaks of three horizons: (1) the immediate material surroundings, (2) the inner existential environment and (3) the absolute horizon. When he speaks as though there are only two horizons, as he does more often, he combines the first two into a single horizon. In *Letters*, pp. 185-87, he writes of four orders (1) the "order of Being," (2) "the order of human freedom, of life, of spirit," (3) the "order of homogenization by violence, perfectly organized impotence and centrally directed desolation and boredom" of man conceived as machine and (4) "the real order of things, of human things above all, the reality around us, its rules, customs, circumstances, relationships."

[8]Havel can certainly be forgiven for his clotted prose; he had to find some way to get his letters past the prison censors. "I soon realized," he wrote in the preface to *Letters to Olga*, "that the more abstract and incomprehensible these meditative letters were, the greater their chance of being sent, since the censors did not permit any comments to be mailed that they could understand. Slowly, I learned to write in a complex, encoded fashion which was far more convoluted than the way I normally write" (*Letters*, p. ix). For example, he explained, "Instead of writing 'regime,' for instance, I would obviously have had to write 'the socially apparent focus of the non-I,' or some such nonsense" (p. 9). On what basis should Heidegger be forgiven?

[9]A shimmering tree also impressed Havel's mentor T. G. Masaryk. "One winter I was on a train going through a tunnel, and just as we came out I caught sight of a tree with all its leaves: the tunnel had protected it. It was gone before I knew it, but it was like a revelation. In that split second I understood pantheism, the divine in nature. Understood it but never accepted it" (Karel Čapek, *Talks with T. G. Masaryk*, trans. Dora Round [New Haven: Catbird Press, 1995], p. 175). Annie Dillard likewise notes the profound effect of "the tree with lights in it" she saw one day as she walked along Tinker Creek (Annie Dillard, *Pilgrim at Tinker Creek* [New York: Bantam Books, 1975], p. 35).

[10]In recent years Havel does occasionally use the term *God* for Being, but then clarifies that he does not have in mind a fully theistic conception (See, for example, Havel's "Faith in the World," p. 53). Robert Pynsent goes to some length to identify the sources of Havel's concept of Being in previous Czech philosophers, but ignores the influence of Heidegger and underemphasizes Havel's general understanding of and utilization of concepts common to traditional Christian theism (*Questions of Identity: Czech and Slovak Ideas of Nationality and Personality* [London: Central European University Press, 1994], pp. 39-42). He makes no mention at all of either phenomenology or the "existential metaexperiences" that Havel credits with revealing and undergirding his understanding of Being.

[11]There is a real problem here, I think, an inconsistency in the application of phenomenological methodology. If Being is the *isness* of what is and Havel concludes that he has been confronted by it as infinite, personal and moral, how can he discern which part of the experience is his own projection and which part is projected by Being? We will deal with this objection in chapter five.

[12]Editors of *The New Age Journal* must have noticed this New Age-sounding language; Havel's lecture "The Philadelphia Liberty Medal" appeared in the September/October 1994 issue, pp. 161-62. Havel also stresses the intentionality of the universe in "Faith in the World," p. 53, where he says that much of our modern problems are due to our loss of "certainty that the Universe, nature, existence and our lives are the work of creation guided by a definite intention, that is, a definite meaning, and follows a definite purpose."

[13]For a presentation and critique of the anthropic principle, see Paul Davies, *God and the New Physics* (New York: Simon & Schuster, 1983), pp. 171-89. For the scientific theory of Gaia, see J. E. Lovelock, *Gaia: A New Look at Life on Earth* (Oxford: Oxford University Press, 1979); for one of many examples of New Age interpretation see Fritjov Capra, *The Turning Point: Science, Society and the Rising Culture* (New York: Bantam Books, 1983), pp. 284-92.

[14]See Pynsent's excellent detailed analysis of Havel's concept of identity, its origins and

its importance in Havel's plays and letters to his wife (*Questions of Identity*, pp. 1-42).

[15]Medical doctor and journalist Lewis Thomas, whose worldview parallels that of Havel, speculates: "I prefer to think of it [human consciousness at death] as somehow separated off at the filaments of its attachment, and then drawn like an easy breath back into the membrane of its origin, a fresh memory for a biospherical nervous system, but I have no data on the matter" (Lewis Thomas, *The Lives of a Cell: Notes of a Biology Watcher* [New York: Bantam Books, 1975], p. 61). Havel has no data on the matter either.

[16]The day I wrote this sentence (January 31, 2000), Havel was once again taken to the hospital with pneumonia. Doctors have warned him that any viral infection is potentially dangerous (Radio Prague, February 2 and 3, 2000). He has since been hospitalized twice again for pneumonia at the end of November 2000 and mid-February 2001 (Radio Prague, November 25 and December 3, 2000, and February 12, 2001).

[17]John Keane, *Václav Havel: A Political Tragedy in Six Acts* (London: Bloomsbury, 1999), p. 364.

[18]Ibid., pp. 494-95.

[19]Roger Scruton, *A Short History of Modern Philosophy from Descartes to Wittgenstein* (London: Routledge, 1984), p. 258. Professor Leopold in *Largo Desolato* also describes phenomenology: "Phenomenology has taught me always to beware of the propositional statement that lies outside demonstrable experience" (*Largo Desolato*, p. 12).

[20]Václav Havel, "The Future of Central Europe," *The New York Review of Books*, March 29, 1990, p. 19.

[21]See, for example, *Summer*, p. 6; and *Art*, pp. 75, 112, 224, 241-42. At the Millennium Summit of the United Nations in 2000, in a near verbatim repeat of his first address to the U. S. Congress, Havel said, "Whenever I encounter any problem of today's civilization, inevitably, I always arrive at one principle theme of human responsibility. This does not mean merely the responsibility of a human being towards his or her own life or survival; towards his or her family; towards his or her company or any other community. It also means responsibility before the infinite and before eternity; in a word, responsibility for the world. Indeed, it seems to me that the most important thing that we should seek to advance in the era of globalization is a sense of global responsibility" ("Address by Václav Havel, President of the Czech Republic, at the Millennium Summit of the United Nations" [September 8, 2000] <www.hrad.cz/president/Havel/speeches/2000/0809_uk>).

[22]"Speech of President of the Czech Republic, Václav Havel, at the International Symposium on Master Jan Hus," Vatican (December 17, 1999) <www.hrad.cz/president/Havel/speeches/1999/1712_uk>.

[23]"Address by Václav Havel, President of the Czech Republic, in Acceptance of an Honorary Degree from the University of Michigan" (September 5, 2000) <www.hrad.cz/president/Havel/speeches/2000/0509_uk>.

[24]"Address by Václav Havel, President of the Czech Republic, on the 150th Anniversary of the Birth of Tomáš Garrigue Masaryk," (March 6, 2000) <www.hrad.cz/president/Havel/speeches/2000/0603_uk>.

[25]See, for example, *Open*, p. 229.

[26]The word *totalitarian* is a vexed term that carries a variety of meanings; I use it as another word for the repressive system that was present in Russia from 1917 to 1989.

Havel uses the term *post-totalitarian* to describe the somewhat less violent but still repressive regime in Czechoslovakia after August 1968 as Russia put an end to "communism with a human face."
[27]*Living*, pp. 62, 118, 137, 152, 183. On patience, see *Art*, pp. 103-8; on sacrifice, see *Art*, pp. 137-38. In his address at Prague Castle (March 7, 2000) honoring the birth of Tomáš Garrigue Masaryk, Havel listed "a spirit embracing humanity, tolerance, decency, openness, discussion, solidarity, kindness, but also firmness" as characteristic of Masaryk and worthy of emulation ("Address by Václav Havel, President of the Czech Republic, on the 150th Anniversary of the Birth of Tomáš Garrigue Masaryk" <www.hrad.cz/president/Havel/speeches/2000/0703_uk>). The previous day in an address on the same topic, he linked Masaryk's virtues to "the factor of eternity, which provides the deepest, and perhaps the only explanation for respect toward a moral order" ("Address by Václav Havel, President of the Czech Republic, on the 150th Anniversary of the Birth of Tomáš Garrigue Masaryk" <www.hrad.cz/president/Havel/speeches/2000/0603_uk>).
[28]Address by Václav Havel, President of the Czech Republic, before the Members of the European Parliament" (February 6, 2000) <www.hrad.cz/president/Havel/speeches/2000/1602_uk>.
[29]"Speech of President of the Czech Republic, Václav Havel, on the occasion of the Presentation of the Christmas Tree for St. Peter's Square to the Holy Father, John Paul II" (December 18, 1999) <www.hrad.cz/president/Havel/speeches/1999/1812_uk>. In a speech at the Vatican the previous day he said, "The idea of a dialogue between different religions is very close to my heart because I see [t]his dialogue as one of the key prerequisites for the process of globalization which permeates all spheres of our civilisation [sic] becoming a process of communication and mutual enrichment, not one of dominance of a single culture over others or one of bartering individuality for universal unification" ("Speech of President of the Czech Republic, Václav Havel, at the International Symposium on Master Jan Hus" <www.hrad.cz/president/Havel/speeches/1999/1712_uk.html>).
[30]Erazim Kohák describes this foundation for morality as "the prereflective certainty of Moravian peasants," as Walter H. Capps points out in his discussion of Havel's philosophy (See Erazim Kohák, *Jan Patočka: Philosophy and Selected Writings* [Chicago: University of Chicago Press, 1989]; and Walter H. Capps, "Interpreting Václav Havel," *Cross Currents*, Fall 1997, p. 308).
[31]See also *Letters*, pp. 53, 149-52. Richard Rorty, in "The End of Leninism: Havel and Social Hope" (*Truth and Progress*, Philosophical Papers, vol. 3 [Cambridge University Press, 1998), p. 236]), looks for a figure who agrees with his view that hope has no metaphysical grounds. He selects Havel and, citing this passage from *Disturbing*, declares that Havel substitutes "groundless hope for theoretical insight." In "The Seer of Prague" (*The New Republic*, July 7, 1991, pp. 37-39), a review of several works by and about Havel's mentor Jan Patočka, Rorty argues for this interpretation. But surely he is incorrect. Undergirding Havel's whole philosophy is the notion of a transcendent in whose presence all reality finds its own being and meaning and hope. Patrick J. Deneen understands Havel correctly, I think, and very differently: "Havel represents more the position that can be described as 'hope without optimism,' a fundamental mistrust in the belief that humans have the ability to solve political and moral problems, but that appeal to a transcendent source—through hope—can serve as a guid-

ing standard, a well as an encouragement to action, but at the same time a source for humility and caution in that attempt" ("The Politics of Hope and Optimism: Rorty, Havel, and the Democratic Faith of John Dewey" [*Social Research,* Summer 1999] <www.findarticles.com/cf_0/2267/2_66/5580613>). Jean Bethke Elshtain, likewise in direct contrast to Rorty, recognizes that Havel's philosophy is grounded ("Don't Be Cruel: Reflections on Rortyian Liberalism," in *The Politics of Irony: Essays in Self-Betrayal,* ed. Daniel W. Conway and John E. Seery [New York: St. Martin's Press, 1992], pp. 214-15).
[32]"Faith in the World," p. 53.

Chapter 4: The Intellectual as Politician

[1]John Keane, *Vàclav Havel: A Political Tragedy in Six Acts* (London: Bloomsbury, 1990). There are yet few analyses in English of Havel's political philosophy. The one I have found most helpful is Vladimir Tismaneanu, *Reinventing Politics: Eastern Europe from Stalin to Havel* (New York: Free Press, 1992), which sets Havel's political writings and life in the context of the past few decades. Among the other significant works are Timothy Garton Ash, "Prague: Intellectuals & Politicians," *The New York Review of Books,* January 12, 1995, pp. 34-41; Walter H. Capps, "Interpreting Václav Havel," *Cross Currents,* Fall 1997, pp. 301-16; Jean Bethke Elshtain, "A Man for This Season: Václav Havel on Freedom and Responsibility," *Perspectives on Political Science,* Fall 1992, pp. 207-11; and Martin J. Matuštík, *Postnational Identity: Critical Theory and Existential Philosophy in Habermas, Kierkegaard and Havel* (London: Guilford, 1993).

[2]Timothy Garton Ash, reflecting on the role of the intellectual, takes exception to Havel: "The intellectual's job is to seek the truth, and then to present it as fully and clearly and interestingly as possible. The politician's job is to work in half-truth"; and again, "It is the role of the thinker or writer who engages in public discussion of issues of public policy, in politics in the broadest sense, while deliberately not engaging in the pursuit of political power." Ash, "Prague: Intellectuals & Politicians," pp. 35-36; Havel responds to Ash in his speech at Victory University, Wellington (*Art* p. 208).

[3]By using the term *postmodern,* Havel does not suggest the approach of Richard Rorty or those commonly taken to be postmodern social pundits; he is rather rejecting Enlightenment rationalism and its modern embodiment in so-called scientific social engineering, and looking instead to an approach that goes to the root of the matter in Being itself, as explained in chapter three.

[4]"Address by Václav Havel, President of the Czech Republic, in Acceptance of an Honorary Degree from Oxford University" (October 22, 1998) <www.hrad.cz/president/Havel/speeches/1998/2210_uk>.

[5]Havel is, of course, well aware of the dangers of the intellectual's arrogance: "Let us remember how many intellectuals helped to create the various modern dictatorships!" (ibid.).

[6]Václav Havel, "Václav Havel Speaks to Fulbrighters," *Fulbright Association Newsletter* 19, no. 4 (1997): 8.

[7]Ivan Klíma in "A Conversation in Prague," in *Writings on the East* (New York: The New York Review of Books, 1990), p. 126. Jacques Rupnik also notes the prevalent "political dimensions" of Havel's plays ("Václav Havel," *Civilization,* April/May 1998, pp.

45-47).

[8]These details and much of the rest of the biographical material on Havel come from Jan Vladislav, "A Short Bio-bibliography of Václav Havel," in *Living*, pp. 295-312.

[9]Walter H. Capps outlines Havel's connection to the rich heritage of Czechoslovak political theory and practice, noting especially the influence on Havel of philosopher and first president of democratic Czechoslovakia Tomáš Garrigue Masaryk and philosophers Edmund Husserl and Jan Patočka ("Interpreting Václav Havel").

[10]Stephen Cohen, "Roses in the Snow," *The New Republic,* January 8-15, 1990, pp. 13-14.

[11]Václav Havel, "The Power of the Powerless," in *Living*, pp. 100-104; Tismaneanu, *Reinventing Politics,* p. 133. See also other dissident essays collected in *Living* and *Open*.

[12]The term "parallel culture" was introduced by Ivan Jirous; Václav Benda speaks of "parallel structures." Havel takes up the theme in both "The Power of the Powerless" and "Six Asides on Culture" (*Living*, pp. 127-35); Tismaneanu discusses the concept at length in *Reinventing Politics,* pp. 133-52.

[13]I owe this observation to my friend and former student Michael Waloschek, a Czech theologian.

[14]Martin J. Matuštík defines a politics as " 'non-political' insofar as it raises the moral imperatives of solidarity and human rights over and against the systematic imperatives of markets and professional politics. Yet it is still 'politics' since it gathers responsible individuals in the multiple public spheres" (*Postnational Identity: Critical Theory and Existential Philosophy in Habermas, Kierkegaard and Havel* [London: Guilford, 1993], p. 197). He calls Havel's view "postnational deliberative democracy" (p. 198).

[15]As a leftist and a Lacanian scholar, Slavoj Zizek, senior researcher at the Institute for Social Studies in Ljubljana, Slovenia, sees Havel's support for the NATO bombing as an indication that Havel's attempt to find a third way between the extremes of communism and capitalism has been "appropriated by the knaves of capitalism" ("Attempts to Escape the Logic of Capitalism," review of *Václav Havel: A Political Tragedy in Six Acts* by John Keane, *London Review of Books,* October 28, 1999 <www.lrb.co.uk/v21/n21/zize2121.htm>).

[16]The most expansive exposition of Havel's dream for Czechoslovakia can be found in his "Beyond the Shock of Freedom" (*Summer,* pp. 102-22).

[17]"A Speech by Václav Havel, the President of the Czech Republic, on the Occasion of a Meeting with the Czech and Slovak Communities in America," at "Václav Havel's Civil Society Symposium" at Macalester College in Minnesota (April 26, 1999) <www.hrad.cz/president/Havel/speeches/1999/2604_uk>.

[18]Václav Havel, "Kosovo and the End of the Nation-State," *The New York Review of Books,* June 6, 1999, p. 6.

Chapter 5: A Critical Analysis of Havel's Worldview

[1]See also *Letters*, pp. 147-48, 190, 375-76.

[2]The most substantial of the few analyses of Havel's philosophic commitments are a two-part essay by Edward E. Ericson Jr., "Václav Havel's Improbable Life," *Books and Culture,* January/February 1999, pp. 14-17, and "That Old-Time Religion," *Books and Culture,* March/April 1999, pp. 17-19; Ericson's "Solzhenitsyn, Havel, and the Twenty-First Century," *Modern Age,* Winter 1999, pp. 3-18; Walter H. Capps, "Interpreting Václav Havel," *Cross Currents,* Fall 1997, pp. 301-16; Martin J. Matuštík,

Postnational Identity: Critical Theory and Existential Philosophy in Habermas, Kierkegaard, and Havel (London: Guilford Press, 1993), pp. 189-201, 247-53; and Jean Bethke Elshtain, "A Man for This Season: Václav Havel on Freedom and Responsibility," *Perspectives on Political Science,* Fall 1992, pp. 207-11.

[3]In my first reading of Havel, I assumed that he holds that Being is omnipotent as well as infinite, omniscient and moral. One reader of my early draft pointed out that the characteristics named in Havel's texts as quoted do not unambiguously include omnipotence. Infinity, however, might be thought to include infinite power, but I do not find Havel saying so explicitly. Without omnipotence Havel's Being could still create and be the ground for morality as well as the final explanation for why things are as they are.

[4]William James, *The Varieties of Religious Experience* (New York: New American Library, 1958), p. 293.

[5]Ibid., pp. 324-25.

[6] Václav Havel, "Last Conversation," in *Good-Bye, Samizdat: Twenty Years of Czechoslovak Underground Writing,* ed. Marketa Goetz-Stankiewicz (Evanston, Ill.: Northwestern University Press, 1992), p. 211.

[7]He quotes from Heidegger in *Letters,* pp. 303, 354.

[8]Roger Scruton, *A Short History of Modern Philosophy from Descartes to Wittgenstein* (London: Routledge, 1984), pp. 259, 264.

[9]Even the rule as stated here is personal (*thou*) as if addressed by another *thou* or *Thou.* See Martin Buber, *I and Thou,* trans. Ronald Gregor Smith (New York: Charles Scribner, 1958).

[10]Peter Kreeft and Ronald K. Tacelli, *Handbook of Christian Apologetics* (Downers Grove, Ill.: InterVarsity Press, 1994), p. 82.

[11]Joseph Brodsky, " 'The Post-Communist Nightmare': An Exchange," *The New York Review of Books,* February 17, 1994, p. 30.

[12]Havel responds to Brodsky, but mentions only the greater evil experienced by Russian dissidents as an explanation for his own less pessimistic view of human nature; he makes no response to Brodsky's more significant charge—about the darkness of the metaphysical order (ibid.).

[13]I have written about this in the chapter on theism in *The Universe Next Door,* 3rd ed. (Downers Grove, Ill.: InterVarsity Press, 1997), pp. 20-38; and in *Why Should Anyone Believe Anything at All?* (Downers Grove, Ill.: InterVarsity Press, 1994).

[14]Marek Mudrik, "Politics and Morality: Václav Havel's Constructive Postmodernism" (master's thesis, Lincoln Christian Seminary, 1999), pp. 50-54.

[15]Steven Erlanger, "One Europe, 10 Years: Gloom in the Castle," *The New York Times,* November 4, 1999.

[16]Jacques Rupnik, "Václav Havel," *Civilization,* April/May 1998, p. 48.

[17]Elizabeth Kiss, "Democracy Without Parties?" *Dissent,* Spring 1992, p. 226. Salvoj Zizek's more recent criticism is even more biting ("Attempts to Escape the Logic of Capitalism," review of *Václav Havel: A Political Tragedy in Six Acts* by John Keane, *London Review of Books,* October 28, 1999 <www.lrb.co.uk/v21/n21/zize 2121.htm>). On the other hand, the viability of Havel's nonpolitical politics is lauded by Vladimir Tismaneanu in *Reinventing Politics: Eastern Europe from Stalin to Havel* (New York: Free Press, 1992), pp. 153-74.

[18]Kiss, "Democracy Without Parties?" p. 230.

[19]Quoted by Erlanger in "One Europe." Havel has also admitted that his failure in the early months of his presidency to reject the building of a nuclear power plant at Temelín—an event that triggered a major protest in Austria—was "his largest political shortcoming" (Prague Radio, October 10, 2000).

[20]Ericson, "Václav Havel's Improbable Life" (p. 17). This and a second essay by Ericson, "That Old-Time Religion," are two of very few analyses of Havel from a Christian perspective. See also Ericson, "Solzhenitsyn, Havel, and the Twenty-First Century"; Capps, "Interpreting Václav Havel"; and Philip Yancey, "The Last Deist," *Christianity Today*, April 5, 1999, p. 88.

[21]James Pitkin, *Prague Post*, August 16, 2000.

[22]Also quoted in "The Philadelphia Liberty Medal," in *Art*, p. 171, and attributed to "a modern philosopher."

[23]Brodsky ("Post-Communist Nightmare"), for example, suggests to Havel that he recommend to his audience the books that he has read (works by Kafka, Faulkner, Proust, Camus) rather than calling them to "new understanding," "global responsibilities" and "pluralistic metaculture." That might at least turn the people of the Czech Republic into "a civilized people."

Chapter 6: The Intellectual as Kafka's Doppelgänger?

[1]The germ of this speech appears ten years earlier in a letter to Olga (November 8, 1980): Havel tells his wife that he has been "delighted" by reading Max Brod's biography of Kafka; it confirms him in his "feeling (hidden, since it might raise suspicions of arrogance) that I somehow understand Kafka better than others, not because I can claim a deeper intellectual insight into his work, but because of an intensely personal and existential understanding of experience that borders on spiritual kinship, if I may put it that way. (I have never much held with theoretical 'interpretations' of Kafka; immensely more important for me was the quite trivial and 'pretheoretical' certainty, as it were, that he was 'right' and that he writes it 'exactly how it is')" (*Letters*, p. 126).

[2]Franz Kafka, *Parables and Paradoxes* (New York: Schocken, 1961), p. 81.

[3]Václav Havel, "Last Conversation," in *Good-Bye, Samizdat: Twenty Years of Czechoslovak Underground Writing*, ed. Marketa Goetz-Stankiewicz (Evanston, Ill.: Northwestern University Press, 1992), p. 212.

[4]See the many confessions of inadequacy in *Letters*, pp. 168, 179, 287, 344, 354; *Open*, p. 3; and *Art*, pp. 70, 75, 198. Even as recently as June 24, 1999, when he delivered a speech in acceptance of the "Open Society" prize, Havel concluded, "I promise you that, as a holder of this award, I shall refrain from inordinate pride and shall not lose anything of the doubts I have had about myself all my life" ("Address by Václav Havel, President of the Czech Republic, in Acceptance of the 'Open Society' Prize" <www.hrad.cz/president/Havel/speeches/1999/2406_uk>).

[5]In August 1979 "A Foreign Ministry official informs Havel while he is in custody that he has been invited to spend a year in New York as a literary adviser on Broadway. Havel refuses to discuss the offer" (Jan Vladislav, "A Short Bio-bibliography of Václav Havel," in *Living*, p. 307).

[6]Havel is indeed very different from Josef K. (or Joseph K., depending on the translation), especially as Pietro Citati so well characterizes him: "Joseph K. is a lonely man, arid, sure, arrogant, presumptuous, certain of his own good faith and his innocence, orderly, aggressive, authoritarian, egotistical, incapable of understanding others,

greedy for earthly success, at times a megalomaniac" (Pietro Citati, *Kafka*, trans. Raymond Rosenthal [New York: Alfred A. Knopf, 1990], p. 139).

[7]Ivan Klíma, "The Swords Are Approaching: Franz Kafka's Sources of Inspiration," in *The Spirit of Prague*, trans. Paul Wilson (New York: Granta, 1994), p. 156-57.

[8]Max Brod, *Franz Kafka: A Biography*, trans. Humphreys Roberts and Richard Winston (New York: Schocken, 1960), pp. 52, 193-95.

[9]Ibid., p. 174.

[10]Brod makes a similar remark about Kafka: "Kafka is always the whole Kafka. Still, we may with some vadidity [sic; validity] affirm that the 'Kafka of the aphorisms' tends more to be a helper and teacher, while the Kafka of the tales and novels tends to be the victim of doubts and self-torture" (ibid., p. 23).

[11]Nelson W. Aldrich, "At the Century's Turn with Václav Havel," *Civilization*, April/May 1998, p. 9.

Bibliography

Books by Havel

Havel, Václav. *The Art of the Impossible: Politics as Morality in Practice*. Translated by Paul Wilson. New York: Alfred A. Knopf, 1997.

————. *Disturbing the Peace: A Conversation with Karel Hvízdala*. Translated by Paul Wilson. New York: Alfred A. Knopf, 1990.

————. *Letters to Olga: June 1979-September 1982*. Translated by Paul Wilson. New York: Henry Holt, 1989.

————. *Living in Truth*. Edited by Jan Vladislav. London: Faber & Faber, 1986.

————. *Open Letters: Selected Writings 1965-1990*. Translated by Paul Wilson. New York: Alfred A. Knopf, 1991.

————. *Summer Meditations*. Translated by Paul Wilson. New York: Alfred A. Knopf, 1992.

Havel, Václav, et al. *The Power of the Powerless: Citizens Against the State in Central-Eastern Europe*. Armonk, N.Y.: M.E. Sharpe, 1985.

Plays by Havel

Havel, Václav. *The Beggar's Opera*. Translated by Paul Wilson. Ithaca: Cornell University Press, 2001.

————. *Largo Desolato*. Translated by Tom Stoppard. New York: Grove Press, 1987.

————. *The Memorandum*. Translated by Vera Blackwell. New York: Grove Weidenfeld, 1980.

————. *Redevelopment or Slum Clearance*. Translated by James Saunders from a literal translation by Marie Winn. London: Faber & Faber, 1990.

————. *Selected Plays 1963-1983*. London: Faber & Faber, 1992. Contains *The Garden Party, The Memorandum, The Increased Difficulty of Concentration, Audience, The Unveiling, Protest*, and *Mistake*.

————. *Temptation*. Translated by Marie Winn. New York: Grove Weidenfeld, 1989.

————. *Three Vaněk Plays*. Translated by George Theiner, Jan Novak and Vera Blackwell. London: Faber & Faber, 1990.

Books and Articles About Havel

Aldrich, Nelson W. "At the Century's Turn with Václav Havel." *Civilization*, April/May 1998, p. 9.

Applebaum, Anne. "Rebel with a Cause." Review of *Václav Havel: A Political Tragedy in Six Acts* by John Keane. *The Weekly Standard*, November 6, 2000 <www.weeklystandard.com/magazine/mag_6_8_00/applebaum_bkart_6_8_00.asp>.

Ash, Timothy Garton. "Eastern Europe: Après Le Déluge, Nous." *The New York Review of Books,* August 16, 1990, pp. 51-64.

———. "Prague: Intellectuals & Politicians." *The New York Review of Books,* January 12, 1995, pp. 34-41.

———. "A Tragedy That Wasn't." Review of *Václav Havel: A Political Tragedy in Six Acts* by John Keane. *Times Literary Supplement,* December 10, 1999, pp. 3-4.

Bayard, Caroline. "The Changing Character of the Prague Intelligentsia." *Telos,* Winter 1992-1993, pp. 131-44.

———. "Postmodern Age: East/West Contrasts." *Philosophy Today,* Winter 1990, pp. 291-302.

Berman, Paul. *A Tale of Two Utopias: The Political Journey of the Generation of 1968.* New York: W. W. Norton, 1996.

Bradbrook, M. C. "Václav Havel's Second Wind." *Modern Drama,* March 1984, pp. 124-32.

Brodsky, Joseph. "'The Post-Communist Nightmare': An Exchange." *The New York Review of Books,* February 17, 1994, p. 30.

Čapek, Karel. *Talks with T. G. Masaryk.* Translated by Dora Round. New Haven, Conn.: Catbird Press, 1995.

Capps, Walter H. "Interpreting Václav Havel." *Cross Currents,* Fall 1997, pp. 301-16.

Carey, Phyllis. "Heaney and Havel: Parables of Politics." In *Seamus Heaney: The Shaping Spirit.* Edited by Catharine Malloy and Phyllis Carey, pp. 137-56. Newark, Del.: University of Delaware Press, 1996.

———. "Living in Lies: Václav Havel's Drama." *Cross Currents,* Summer 1992, pp. 201-11.

Civilization, April/May 1998.

Cohen, Stephen. "Roses in the Snow." *The New Republic,* January 8-15, 1990, pp. 13-14.

Day, Barbara. *The Velvet Philosophers.* London: Claridge, 1999.

Deneen, Patrick. "The Politics of Hope and Optimism: Rorty, Havel, and the Democratic Faith of John Dewey." *Social Research,* Summer 1999 <www.findarticles.com/cf_0/2267/2_66/5580613>.

Draper, Theodore. "The End of Czechoslovakia." *The New York Review of Books,* January 28, 1993, pp. 20-26.

Elshtain, Jean Bethke. "Don't Be Cruel: Reflections on Rortyian Liberalism." In *The Politics of Irony: Essays in Self-Betrayal.* Edited by Daniel W. Conway and John E. Seery, pp. 199-217. New York: St. Martin's Press, 1992.

———. "A Man for This Season: Václav Havel on Freedom and Responsibility." *Perspectives on Political Science,* Fall 1992, pp. 207-11.

———. "Politics Without Cliché." *Social Research,* Fall 1993, pp. 433-44.

Ericson, Edward E. Jr. "Solzhenitsyn, Havel, and the Twenty-First Century." *Modern Age,* Winter 1999, pp. 3-18.

———. "That Old-Time Religion." *Books and Culture,* March/April 1999, pp. 17-19.

———. "Václav Havel's Improbable Life." *Books and Culture,* January/February 1999, pp. 14-17.

Erlanger, Steven. "One Europe, 10 Years: Gloom in the Castle." *The New York Times,* November 4, 1999.

Gellner, Ernest. "The Price of Velvet: On Thomas Masaryk and Václav Havel." Review of *Summer Meditations* by Václav Havel. *Telos,* Winter 1992-1993, pp. 183-92.

Goetz-Stankiewicz, Marketa. "Ethics at the Crossroads: The Czech 'Dissident Writer' as Dramatic Character." *Modern Drama,* March 1984, pp. 112-23.

―――. *The Silenced Theatre: Czech Playwrights Without a Stage.* Toronto: University of Toronto Press, 1979.

―――. "Václav Havel: A Writer for Today's Season," *World Literature Today,* Summer 1981, pp. 389-93.

―――, ed. *Good-Bye, Samizdat: Twenty Years of Czechoslovak Underground Writing.* Evanston, Ill.: Northwestern University Press, 1992.

Goetz-Stankiewicz, Marketa, and Phyllis Carey, eds. *Critical Essays on Václav Havel.* New York: G. K. Hall & Co., 1999.

Keane, John. *Václav Havel: A Political Tragedy in Six Acts.* London: Bloomsbury, 1999.

Kiss, Elizabeth. "Democracy Without Parties?" *Dissent,* Spring 1992, pp. 226-31.

Klíma, Ivan. *The Spirit of Prague.* Translated by Paul Wilson. New York: Granta, 1994.

Kohák, Erazim. *Jan Patočka: Philosophy and Selected Writings.* Chicago: University of Chicago Press, 1989.

Kriseová, Edá. *Václav Havel: The Authorized Biography.* New York: St. Martin's Press, 1993.

Matuštík, Martin J. *Postnational Identity: Critical Theory and Existential Philosophy in Habermas, Kierkegaard and Havel.* London: Guilford, 1993.

Pynsent, Robert B. *Questions of Identity: Czech and Slovak Ideas of Nationality and Personality.* London: Central European University Press, 1994.

Rorty, Richard. "The End of Leninism, Havel and Social Hope." In *Truth and Progress,* Philosophical Papers, vol. 3, pp. 228-43. Cambridge: Cambridge University Press, 1998.

―――. "The Seer of Prague." *The New Republic,* July 7, 1991, pp. 37-39.

Rupnik, Jacques. "Václav Havel," *Civilization,* April/May 1998, pp. 45-49.

Sire, James W. "An Open Letter to Václav Havel." *Crux,* June 1991, pp. 9-14.

―――. "Playwright, Dissident, Czech President . . . Who Is This Man?" Review of *Václav Havel: A Political Tragedy in Six Acts* by John Keane. *Christianity Today,* January 31, 2000 <www.christianitytoday.com/ct/2000/105/11.0.html>.

Tismaneanu, Vladimir. *Reinventing Politics: Eastern Europe from Stalin to Havel.* New York: Free Press, 1992.

Whipple, Tim D. *After the Velvet Revolution: Václav Havel and the New Leaders of Czechoslovakia Speak Out.* New York: Freedom House, 1991.

Williams, Kieran. "Apologists Rejoice!" Review of *Václav Havel: A Political Tragedy in Six Acts* by John Keane. *Central Europe Review,* November 29, 1999 <www.cereview.org/99/23/williams23.html>.

Wilson, Paul. "Czechoslovakia: The Pain of Divorce." *The New York Review of Books,* December 17, 1992, pp. 69-75.

Zizek, Slovoj. "Attempts to Escape the Logic of Capitalism." Review of *Václav Havel: A Political Tragedy in Six Acts* by John Keane. *London Review of Books,* October 28, 1999 <www.lrb.co.uk/v21/n21/zize2121.htm>.

Index